Where is Language?

Overdue items may incur charges as published in the current Schedule of Charges.

L21

Where is Language?

An Anthropologist's Questions on Language, Literature and Performance

By Ruth Finnegan

Bloomsbury Academic
An imprint of Bloomsbury Publishing Plc

B L O O M S B U R Y
LONDON • NEW DELHI • NEW YORK • SYDNEY

Bloomsbury Academic

An imprint of Bloomsbury Publishing Plc

50 Bedford Square	1385 Broadway
London	New York
WC1B 3DP	NY 10018
UK	USA

www.bloomsbury.com

BLOOMSBURY and the Diana logo are trademarks of Bloomsbury Publishing Plc

First published 2015

© Ruth Finnegan, 2015

Ruth Finnegan has asserted her right under the Copyright, Designs and Patents Act, 1988, to be identified as Author of this work.

British Library Cataloguing-in-Publication Data

A catalogue record for this book is available from the British Library.

ISBN: HB: 978-1-4725-9092-3
PB: 978-1-4725-9093-0
ePDF: 978-1-4725-9095-4
ePub: 978-1-4725-9094-7

Library of Congress Cataloging-in-Publication Data

A catalog record for this book is available from the Library of Congress.

Typeset by Fakenham Prepress Solutions, Fakenham, Norfolk, NR21 8NN
Printed and bound in India

To the evergreen memory of Gerhardt Baumann who would have liked and, as is right, argued with this book. We will never forget you.

CONTENTS

PREFACE

What could be greater than linguistic expression for narrating the deep story of our identities, clothing our emotions in beautiful language, using the modalities of our bodies to communicate and embellish our words, formulating the lyrics of songs or our dreams into narrative? And yet, like 'time' for Saint Augustine, what, when we come to think of it, is so little understood?

A host of puzzles face us when we do come to think about it. Do we, in our Western way, exaggerate the significance of what we term language – above all, our particular form of language, alphabetic literacy, 'the tool of conquest'? Are not other modes as profound, perhaps 'divine' as some would put it, and, above all, is it only a Western cultural trait to see verbalizing as the greatest art of all?

We need a more multiplex, challenging, but more contextually situated understanding of language, literature and performance. And if the search involves challenging some accepted stereotypes, this is scarcely too high a price to pay for a greater understanding, controversial as it may be, of phenomena so apparently crucial to our humanity.

The present volume represents the fruit of a lifetime's puzzling over the subject, reinforced by my desire – need – to set the issues, as far as in me lie, in some kind of cross-cultural perspective. So I start here, as do most scholars, anthropologists included (we are not just creatures of fieldwork or the exotic), from a closely interested reading of the literature, beginning with the ancient classics, followed by intensive reading and fieldwork in three continents. The results have also drawn (of course) on primary evidence, including the field research of both myself and others, interpreted in the light of the comparative material from throughout the world and the centuries. The two inform each other.

ACKNOWLEDGEMENTS

Some of the ideas (but not necessarily the expression) behind the account here have, not unnaturally, appeared in other publications before now, although their conflation and articulation are unique to this volume. So let me, as is courteous, mention in particular *Compétence et Performance*, Karthala; *International Journal of Learning*; *Language Description and Documentation*; *Newsletter of British Association for Applied Linguistics*; *Oral Tradition*; *Palavra Cantada: Ensaios sobre Poesia, Música e Voz*, 7 Letras; *Consumption and Everyday Life*, Sage; *Technology, Literacy and the Evolution of Society*, Erlbaum; *The Art of English: Literary Creativity*, Palgrave Macmillan.

On a more personal level I owe great gratitude to the librarians and colleagues at my long-time institution the Open University, of which I am proud to have been a founder member (too many to name individually, but you know who you are – still so kind even to an old lag like myself). My thanks too to the unknown readers for the press who not only encouraged me to persevere but markedly improved the clarity and coherence of this offering. Of other individuals – again too many to name – let me merely thank my dear husband David, always beside me, and, in abiding memory, Gerhardt Baumann to whom this book is dedicated; he would no doubt have fixed on all its minor inaccuracies (I hope there are not too many) and any typos that have escaped the excellent Bloomsbury process – but would nevertheless have welcomed it with his inimitable smile.

1

What is the art of language?

It is common to assume we know what language is and what is needed to capture and describe it; hence, by implication, what 'language' in essence is. But there are many contending theories, too easily forgotten in the understandable rush to document and describe. These need to be considered at the outset, above all the performance approach to linguistic action entailed in pragmatic perspectives, and the issue of how and for whom linguistic accounts are constructed in the first place.

I too was once confident of what 'language' was, where its boundaries lay, and hence what might count as data for documenting it. But I am no longer sure. Nor am I clear where information about a given language should be found, or how, by, and for whom a language should be documented.

My uncertainties are founded in my own puzzles over the many years that I've worked, mainly as an anthropologist, on aspects of unwritten literature, performance and communication, based both in comparative reading and fieldwork in Africa and Britain (Finnegan 1967, 1970, 1977, 1988, 1989, 1992, 1998, 2002, 2007). Within that limited experience, I find that the issues I have confronted are unexpectedly (to me) relevant for the understanding of the nature of language and how to capture it, whether in our contemporary world or in the so-called 'vanishing' cultures.

What I offer here are some informal reflections, not any pretence of a scholarly or theoretical disquisition.[1] I write not as a specialist linguist nor

---

1 Given the personal setting of this introductory chapter there are many references to my own work, unclothed furthermore by the decencies of systematic citations throughout. But since my personal experience is of course interrelated with changing and contending approaches to language and communication, let me mention that works I have at various times found especially illuminating include Austin 1962, Bakhtin 1986, Bauman 1977, Bauman and Sherzer 1989, Bauman and Briggs 1990, 2003, Clark 1996, Cummings 2010, Dalby 1999/2000, Duranti 2004, Gippert et al. 2006, Hanks 1996, Harris 1987, 1998, Harris and Wolf 1998, Hodge and Kress 1993, Hymes 1977, Robinson 2006, Tracey 1999, Verschueren 2009, Verschueren and Östman 2009. Some issues touched on here are considered in more fully referenced framework in Finnegan 2002/14, 2007.

as someone with any expertise in documenting languages, but merely about my experience of becoming increasingly doubtful of my initially confident assumptions about just where in the great spectrum of human communicating and expression we are to find 'language'.

My first degree was in Classics – Greek and Latin. At that point I 'knew' what language was – or rather, I didn't need to know because it seemed self-evident. It was what came in written texts. Written texts were the prime sources that had come down to us from classical antiquity, transmitted in the manuscript tradition and with, of course, no audio records of speech. The texts we read and studied were wonderful and enriching, covering a wide range of genres: literary, historical, epistolatory, oratorical, lyrical and much else. Both drawn from and supporting this corpus of texts was the extensive apparatus of vocabulary, of grammar and of syntax, all once again encapsulated in writing in the form of dictionaries of words (usually offering equivalencies in some European language) and accounts of grammatical and syntactical rules. The written words, organized in the correct classic formulations – that was ultimately what language was.

This emphasis on the textual and written was not totally unqualified. Archaeology – the study of material remains – played a part, and some scholars (like Eduard Fraenkel from Germany) went beyond the printed page to read aloud a Catullus love poem or (W. B. Stanford from Ireland) engaged with the acoustic dimensions of Greek lyric meters. There was an established tradition, though not within the examination curriculum, of live performances of Greek plays or of reading Homer aloud. But the paradigm was indubitably of the centrality of written text both as the object of what was studied and the medium in which such study was appropriately expressed.

From this viewpoint, documenting a little-known language (i.e. one unwritten-about philologically) would entail finding and pinning down its essential constituent: texts that could be read, analysed and form the basis for identifying underlying rules. The texts might have to be snared by transcribing spoken words into writing. But ultimately those resultant scripts, together with a similar scholarly apparatus as for classical languages, would form the necessary documentation data. Language was capturable and realized in the communication technology dominant in the mid-twentieth century and earlier – writing – and it was ultimately there that the data could be recognized.

Emerging doubts …

Things began to look different when, as a graduate, I embarked on anthropological studies, followed ineluctably by my first piece of fieldwork. This was in the early 1960s among a people called the Limba, in northern Sierra Leone. My focus came to be on their stories and story-telling, an interest that followed on well from my enthusiasm for literary texts in my earlier studies. I was hugely impressed by the many story-telling performances I experienced there and wanted to make that aspect of Limba culture the central core for my thesis and subsequent publications.

My initial presupposition was that the way to study these stories – and most certainly the way to present them in my doctoral dissertation – was to capture them as written text. That, after all, was surely where their reality lay, and the medium in which I and other scholars possessed the necessary analytic tools. There seemed no other proper way to pin them down for scholarly study.

So some of the stories I transformed, directly, into script by taking them down from dictation. Many others I recorded on one of the (relatively) portable tape recorders then available. The obvious next step was to transcribe from tape into written lines on a page in similar format to the classical texts I and others were accustomed to.

My thesis could then take the familiar form of introductory background and analysis followed by the key data: parallel texts in Limba and English translation. It consequently ran to three large volumes (I still remember their weight as I lugged the required three copies of each through Oxford by bicycle, then up the steps to the examinations schools). I assumed – as, apparently, did my examiners – that the substantive data, the corpus of texts, had to be there in my presentation.

But there was a problem. I had been greatly struck by the richness and subtlety of these narrations, and in my thesis tried to convey something of their artistry. But that had somehow melted away in the stories I presented. At one point, trying to demonstrate why I was so enthusiastic, I showed one of the texts to a friend from my classical days, expecting him to be impressed. He read through and rejoined – politely – 'Oh yes, another of those charming African animal tales', to my mind missing all its wonders.

The point is of course only too obvious, though it took me some time to appreciate it fully. The reality lay in the performance. It was this that the written texts had failed to capture. They missed the subtle characterizations, the drama, the way the tellers used volume, pitch, tempo, repetition, emphasis, dynamics, silence, timbre, onomatopoeia, and a whole plethora of non-verbal indications to convey humour, pathos, irony, atmosphere … The written forms could never replicate the ideophones that peppered the tellings – vivid little mini-images in sound and more than sound. Nor could unilinear textual layout show the many-voiced interaction and co-construction by the audience as they joined in songs led by the narrator or reacted with horror or laughter to key turns in the tale. Nor, either, did it capture the Limba practice of picking out one among the audience as the 'replier' – a second voice to give special support, prompting, echoing and, where needed, exaggerated reactions and response. Compressing this multidimensional and multi-participant performance within the narrow one-voiced medium of writing was to miss its substance.

I soon discovered that similar patterns were found elsewhere – obvious once you look, but for long concealed from me (and others) by the presupposed centrality of written text. The study of oral poetry, performance, and 'oral literature' more generally, hammered home the same point. Both in Africa and further afield, those creating performed literary art deploy not just writable words but a vast range of non-verbalized auditory devices of which those conventionally captured in written text, such as rhyme, alliteration and rhythm, are only a small sample. The wondrously varied expressive resources of the human voice are exploited for multifarious delivery modes, varying with genre, situation or performer: spoken, sung, recited, intoned, shouted, whispered, carried by single or multiple or alternating voices. Not just in faraway places but in the spoken and sung forms nearer home too, there turned out to be near-infinite combinations of vocal expression and auditory resources of which most escape from view on the written page.

I had to conclude, then, that the core lay not in written text after all but in the performance. And that included the setting, the delivery, and not just the 'lead' speaker but the full range of participants. All this showed up the contentious nature of my earlier 'language-as-written-text' model. This was reinforced by ongoing trends in the study of verbal expression, not least the performance-oriented approaches and ethnography of speaking in folklore and anthropology – stressing performance and process rather than text and product – as well as more recent developments in linguistic anthropology, sociolinguistics and performance studies. At the same time interdisciplinary interests in oral performance and in 'orality' more generally were, and are, flourishing, opening up a new vision of the nature of human communication and expression previously concealed by the focus on the written.

This turned me towards seeing language as ultimately something spoken, performed, oral. It no longer seemed to be existent essentially in written text but in active performance and interaction. And if so, language documentation would have to be approached very differently than from the familiar written-text perspective. For it would have to focus on audio, not just written, materials, and to include records and analyses of oral performances and (where relevant) their multiplicity of overlapping participants. Such data would not only count, but be essential.

Plunging into the 'oral'

Acknowledging the limitations of a written-text model of language is hopefully by now scarcely problematic. Audio recordings are nowadays widely accepted as a regular (though perhaps not universal) part of serious language documentation. I would like to add two further comments, however, about the implications.

First, a qualification. The move away from the written to the 'oral' sometimes jumps to the opposite extreme, envisaging the spoken as somehow the bedrock, natural, traditional, to be set against the artificial imposition of writing. A seminal Western myth sometimes lurks behind this, constantly challenged but also constantly recycled. In ways more fully explored in the next chapter, this posits a fundamental opposition between two mutually exclusive types of social and cognitive organization: the one literate, rational, scientific, civilized, Western, modern; the other communal, emotional, non-scientific, traditional, primitive – and oral. This has underpinned a trend to mystify 'orality' and the 'oral' as if something distinctive and separate: characteristic of a culture belonging prototypically to the 'them' of far away or long ago and one in which writing, even if in certain respects present, is intrinsically alien (and to be ignored). This is a set of assumptions I have long found myself struggling against and one which no doubt also crops up – controversially – in certain approaches to language documentation.

In other ways, however, the analysis of the oral and performed dimensions of language has, paradoxically, not been taken far enough. The vocabulary to capture the amazing use of the voice with its huge range of subtleties is relatively little developed, and the sonic elements of language are still often sidelined. But if we are to document the auditory practice of language, then the data to count would need to cover not just rules about phonetics, word forms or (limited elements of) prosody but its active sonic realization in such features as, for example, pacing and speed, volume, pitch, melody, rhythm, onomatopoeia, voice quality, timbre, mood, mix with other voices and sounds – or silences, distancing, vocalized sounds like sobs, sighs or laughter ... and so much else. Data about tone or prosody would have to include not just smaller units like words, phrases or sentences but also the sonic patternings of larger chunks and of speech genres more widely. It's true that such elements sometimes get mentioned under the heading of 'paralinguistic' or 'extralinguistic' elements, but in an oral-performance model of language these are not supplementary extras but intrinsic. A Martian anthropologist might well be puzzled by a demarcation which included some auditory elements in the delineation of language but excluded others which can equally form part of both the conventions and the unique personality communicated through human vocal utterance.

So though the importance of audio features may now be increasingly taken for granted in documenting languages, helped by the audio technologies which now facilitate the recording, storage and accessing of such data, has this yet been fully followed through? Documenting the oral is inevitably enormously complex; nor, despite the wizardries of modern technology, have we really developed adequate techniques, vocabularies or perhaps concepts to fully capture and analyse these inevitably more fleeting and temporal performed features.

Small wonder, perhaps, that the written model of language is so extraordinarily persistent, with its implicit suggestion that data doesn't quite 'exist' until it is reduced to, transcribed as, transformed into, or analysed through the spatial solidity of writing and print. As Hodge and Kress well put it: 'The distinctive resources of spoken communication which are not transcribed are eliminated from linguistic theory' (1993: 11). Even when we accept a view of language as sounded and performed, we still too often fall comfortably back into a model in which the true reality – and the key data – reside in visually written textualizations rather than vocal enunciation.

Cognitive models

My Limba fieldwork brought me face to face not just with story-telling performance but also with the active way that Limba speakers used vocal utterances to do things. This, I gradually discovered, ran counter to a further implicit model of language that, if only in a vague and muddled way, I had also had at the back of my mind.

This was a set of somewhat contradictory and elusive assumptions, which could indeed be split apart but which nevertheless tended to come together in a kind of general mindset which I'd sum up under the label of 'cognitive'. Basically I pictured language as something essentially mental, rational, decontextualized. Language was to do with mind and meaning, and its central function was referential. Artistry and rhetoric were secondary embellishments only to be considered once the core prose and information-bearing elements were grasped. Language might or might not constitute an independent rule-governed system existing autonomously in its own right – I vaguely assumed that it did – but it certainly could be assumed to have a structure that could be abstracted from the messiness of context, usage and social action or experience.

Of course I should already have known that this was not the whole story, both from my own experience and from my encounter with the multiplicity of classical genres. Even so, I was still somehow steeped in that set of preconceptions. It had been reinforced in part by the legacy of logical positivism still influential in my undergraduate years at Oxford (though tempered by Austin's lectures on 'performative utterances' which were much to influence me subsequently). More radically, as I came to realize, it was a continuance of an ideology powerful in Western thought over several centuries which asserted the rationality of language and its relation to science, objectivity, civilization, literacy and, ultimately, the achievements of the West.

In some ways it was a serviceable model for a field situation. My language learning had indeed initially relied on the presupposition of a systematic vocabulary and grammar that I could learn independently of the pressures of spoken situations. There was a short missionary-compiled Limba dictionary, a couple of translated gospels, and two short articles based on data from an overseas Limba visitor, elicited and analysed by a linguist (Jack Berry) then at the School of Oriental and African Studies in London, all of which I found hugely helpful.

This all fitted both my preconceptions about the systematized and meaning-carrying nature of language and where to find data about it, and my conviction that meaning could be conveyed cross-culturally and out of context. Language as the repository of thought offered the potential for its 'translation', a channel by which minds could be brought into contact across space and time. It was through language that Limba stories could be transported to others as text – something which I indeed aspired to do through my verbal translations.

My aim was not to document language as such, whether that of Limba speakers or any others. But if it had been, I would doubtless have started from the assumption that the core data would be found in the information-carrying forms, in 'plain prose' sentences and the logical structure underlying them; also that I would have to produce clear translations and word-for-word equivalences to enable the direct transference of meaning from this lesser-known culture into some accessible European language.

Greater experience of Limba life somewhat undermined that set of preconceptions. I could not really miss the way Limba speakers used speaking as organized action and performance rather than, or as well as, for conveying meaning. They used language to do things rather than just describe them: to recognize and forge relationships, ratify contracts, issue orders, assert a position, strike an attitude, show off as performer.

Further, in some interchanges, and even in some Limba stories, the cognitive 'content' as it were – the meaning I had assumed I could transfer – was not after all the only, or in some cases even apparently the most important, element. I think, for example, of one ridiculous short story I recorded about a fictional character called Daba, an incorrigible snuff-taker. All that happened in it was that Daba went round the local chiefs badgering them to give him vast quantities of snuff, then finally overreached himself by taking a huge sniff and falling down dead: nothing to it really. And yet this was hugely successful with the audience, who were rolling with merriment. It was told by one of the most admired local tellers and was among the liveliest narrations I encountered, subtle as well as hilarious. Its success lay not in its plot but in the teller's brilliant performance and the audience's active co-creation and singing as Daba sniffed and sniffed again, also in the narrator's skill in exploiting their shared knowledge of local personalities, satirized as Daba goes the round of the chiefs, and of the ludicrous way some people carry on, held up to mockery in Daba's absurdly extreme personality.

I had also rather assumed that in focusing on stories, I had managed to select a core linguistic genre: narrative, close to 'ordinary speech' and thus somehow basic in a way that their songs and more overtly 'artistic' behaviour were not. I tacitly congratulated myself on that, feeling it took me direct into something primary about their language. But I came to acknowledge that story-telling was no more nor less 'natural' than any other genre. It too had its own speech conventions. Nor was there anything special about either narrative or (so-called) 'prose' that gave them any more seminal or objective status than anything else. All cultures, I had to accept, recognize a variety of 'speech genres', as Bakhtin (1986) famously had it, each with their own poetics.

Not that everything about a cognitive view of language seemed wrong. But both from fieldwork experience and more comparative work on literacy and communication media more generally, I became doubtful how far that set of preconceptions could adequately illuminate either the Limba experience or human culture as it was realized in practice. And if so, the data necessary for documenting a language would seem to involve not primarily matters to do with 'its' abstract linguistic system, translateable cognitive meaning or supposedly 'primary' forms such as narrative or conversation, but data from and about the full range of recognized genres. It would have to cover the near-unending and diverse ways people used and enacted language: for art, action, reflection, play or whatever.

An impossible project? But might aiming at anything less risk invoking a seriously incomplete model of language?

Where are the boundaries?

And amid all those puzzles, I have also become unclear how to divide language from other (but are they other?) modes of human expression. One uncertainty still dogging me is the relation between music and language. Some cases are perhaps clearly one or the other, but where, if anywhere, does the line come?

Take intonation. I originally assumed that this was to do with individual words or sentences and, as such, a relatively accepted, if limited, dimension in some (perhaps not all) approaches to language. Thus, in the Limba stories I recorded, I took it that intonation was effective in particular phrases and how they were delivered, but not of much interest in the narration more widely. But I changed my mind when, unexpectedly, I was played an audio recording of a Mossi story from some hundreds of miles away, in a very different West African language. I knew no Mossi, so listened to the sounds. I was amazed to hear familiar intonational and rhythmic patterning in long passages of the telling. It could have been a Limba performance. I had not noticed before how part of the characterization of the genre was its sonic shaping.

A similar point applies in the comparative study of oral poetry. Not only are there many varieties of rhythmically and sonically patterned delivery, delineating both particular generic conventions and unique performance attributes, but some poems are performed in a way that means they could equally well be described either as 'sung poetry' or as 'vocal music' – or, indeed, as 'song'. In these performed genres, enacted by single or multiple voices, sometimes instrumentally embellished too, should I really be endeavouring to separate 'linguistic' from 'musical' elements, and if so how? The same applied in the urban music-making I studied in both Fiji and England – tearing apart the 'song texts' (as, like many other scholars, I often found myself doing ...) was in practice to mangle the songs' reality.

It is true that in some cultural contexts a music/language division seems self-evident. In the European high art song tradition of 'text-setting', words and music are indeed in a sense separated, then artificially, as it were – or at any rate, by artifice – brought together. But it has in fact been urged for some time that the apparent distinction between language and music would be better represented as a continuum rather than dichotomy (for the relatively few analyses of this issue see List 1963 and, more recently, Feld and Fox 1994, Banti and Giannatasio 2004, Finnegan 2006). In practice it is near impossible to drive a clear wedge between the multifarious modes of vocal expression: speaking, intoning, chanting, recitative, melodic singing, and so much else. Ethnocentric too, given that the classifications of different cultures vary. Even in Western experience the classical Greek *mousiké* originally had a different coverage from the modern 'music', for it encompassed what we would now differentiate as music, poetry and dance, while the medieval *musica* covered spoken as well as sung performance, with little idea, apparently, of words and music as 'separate expressive media that one could choose to unify or not' (Treitler 2003: 47).

Indeed, even in modern times can one really divide up the music and the language of vocal performance, whether T. S. Eliot declaiming his poetry, Edith Sitwell chanting her *Façade*, a fine reading of a Shakespeare sonnet or a contemporary rap or dub performance? All these resonate through the sounding voice as people deploy an unending wealth of sonic resources in their vocal utterances.

So should the melodic and rhythmic qualities of performed vocal utterances – what some might separate out as 'music' – be appropriate data for language documentation? How far to include them depends on where and whether we are prepared to draw a boundary between music and language – and that, it seems, is far from unambiguous or culturally neutral.

Problems about boundaries do not just relate to audition, as is sometimes assumed from too enthusiastically embracing the concept of 'oral'/'orality'. As I learnt from watching Limba narrators, performers can also draw strikingly on visual resources. Not just in Limba contexts – the setting which first most directly alerted me – but, I now realize, in communication more generally, people make use of gesture, facial expression, eye glances, bodily orientation, demeanour, movements, material artefacts. To learn a language fluently includes mastering the appropriate visible actions belonging to particular genres or situations. So where do you draw the line?

The question is raised particularly by gesture. In many standard approaches this is set apart from language. But recent studies of the intimate ways gestures are systematically coordinated with speech (see for example Haviland 2004, Kendon 2000, McNeill 2000) have raised the question of whether the boundaries of language should be widened to include them. Here again, modern communication technologies have expanded our capacity to capture – and thus notice – the significance of moving images, endowing them with a solidity concealed when we limit ourselves to script-based tools. So is it justifiable or not to claim that any language could be fully documented without data on the uses of gestures?

Once we go beyond models of language as centred on written text or on abstract or cognitive systems, and consider practice and performance, it also becomes inescapable that human communicating is commonly multi-sensory. As well as audio and visual elements – many-sided as these already are – tactile and somatic elements may be in play too, as in the danced and embodied movements that characterize some genres and performances. The physical setting and spatial arrangements can carry their resonances too, not least in the multisensory proxemic relations between participants. Multimodality may be more to the fore in some genres than in others. But where it is a feature, should we screen out such data by implicitly invoking a model of language where such dimensions do not really count?

I have also been intrigued by the diverse ways in which representation in other modes or materials – not just music or gesture – can work alongside or be variously linked or paralleled with speech. Pictures, sculptures, drumming, sign languages, tactile tools, web representations – there are a host of complex interrelationships. These too may in any given case be closely tied into verbal usage and arguably count among the data that should count. But they are likely to work – and be conceptualized – differently in different situations and cultures, and a link seen as self-evident in one setting to be highly problematic in others.

In the case of the visible marks labelled as 'writing' there might seem no argument; these surely are inextricably tied into 'language'. But the comparative study of literacy has raised two issues for me. First, insofar as we do recognize close speech-writing ties, then data about this particular form of material representation is indeed relevant in documenting the language. At one point the established presupposition – by which I was implicitly swayed during earlier fieldwork but revised when I came to study literacy more directly – seemed to be that whereas written forms were self-evidently basic in 'developed' languages, elsewhere writing was somewhat intrusive and alien. If so, perhaps it did not really count among the authentic data for some kinds of languages? On the other hand, if written forms are in fact current now, should they not be considered relevant for the present linguistic situation? I (and many others) would probably now say that they should, and would also want to include in the data not just oral/written contrasts but their interactions and, perhaps, interpenetrations. But then that, of course, is again to make particular assumptions about the scope of language.

That leads to a second question. In Western contexts it has seemed self-evident that language can reasonably be identified, in broad terms, as speech and writing (and in particular alphabetic writing): the link seems a natural one. But to take for granted that these two media have a given one-to-one equivalence is perhaps cross-culturally problematic. And if writing is to count, then what about the other modes and media that are in one way or another closely linked into speech – pictorial, material, tactile or whatever, varying in different cultures? Should they too be considered as potentially relevant data?

So does language turn out to spill across all the resources that human beings so wonderfully exploit in their communication and expression alongside, or intertwined with, speech? For practical purposes the bound-aries have to be drawn somewhere no doubt. But to do so is unavoidably to take up a particular stance and thus become liable to criticism as incomplete, lop-sided or ethnocentric. For wherever they are drawn is to make debateable assumptions about the nature and limits of 'language'.

Who should capture 'a language'?

My puzzles about language also extend into queries about who or what should be involved in providing and collecting the data.

I can bypass the well-worked issue of just where the boundaries of 'a' language can be set, since the older picture of unitary and exclusive languages seems to have been replaced by a more realistic awareness of relativity and diversity. But I would like to comment on the commonly-used and partly analogous term 'speech community'.

In many ways I find this concept helpful, especially for its focus not on abstract systems but on people and usage. But 'community' is itself a controversial and elusive concept. It raises questions of who demarcates and draws its edges and whether these are defined in terms of, say, location, identity, perception (and whose perceptions?). It has long been tempting to see something dubbed as a 'community' as homogeneous and bounded – when in practice it might equally well be heterogeneous, made up of perhaps warring interests, without clear boundaries and by no means necessarily permanent. There is an additional pull to romanticize 'communities' that consist of people who can be thought of as somehow other – minorities, far away, long ago, or, alternatively, in some way an issue on the political horizon. Sometimes the term evokes that still emotive image of the homogenous, unchanging, and romantic past. In my Limba fieldwork I was less critical than I should have been of the temptation of positing generalized 'traditional' patterns – even though I knew there were differences in different areas and that 'the Limba' had been demarcated by colonial administrators and others as speaking one language (and 'hence' comprising one tribe) despite the many dialects, multilingualisms and overlaps with surrounding and intermingled speakers of differently labelled languages.

Such images are the more entrancing with a 'speech community' that can be seen as the repository of an endangered language – an understandably value-laden topic. But does that perhaps make it all the more important for the documentation to tell it how it is – and how people use it now not in some notionally pure and uncontaminated past? Should the data include the diversities and contradictions, mixtures of perceptions from past and present and from differing perspectives, the invented 'traditions', unequal powers, warring viewpoints? And since it can be argued that few 'speech communities' are truly monolingual or culturally uniform (especially perhaps if their language is now 'endangered') will the data include the overlaps and interactions with other languages, perhaps both written and spoken, and what might once have been dismissed as 'hybrid' genres or speech? Schooled forms, popular novels, influences from 'European' genres, translations, bilingual forms, writing – all may now in practice be part of the reality of (some?) people's lives, not easily to be discounted as aberrant or 'alien'. The study of familiar Western languages takes for granted that cultures, communities and languages change and interact with others. Should we demand something different, some frozen essence, once a language is classed as endangered? So too with the practices of translation, of language-switching and interpenetration, global interactions, young versus old – none of these are necessarily 'abnormal' or irrelevant. If the way 'a language' exists is in how people speak, enact, create, change and manipulate verbal resources, then the data to count might need to come from that full range, not from some idealized atemporal prior state (once again illustrating how delineating both 'speech community' and data may be inseparable from assumptions about the nature of 'language').

This also affects the question of who provides the description and decides what it means. The older images of the homogeneous and unchanging 'tribe', 'language' or 'community' envisaged everyone as essentially sharing a common tradition. So, in anthropology as in language documentation, it seemed to matter little who you got your information from. The 'myths of the Bongo Bongo' (or whoever) could be elicited equally well from any member of the group. Now we are more critical. We are sensitive, hopefully, to change, manipulation, disagreements, inventions, power relations. Like others, I have also become increasingly aware of the extent to which the processes of dictation, transcription, translation and recording are not mechanical but socially and individually shaped (Finnegan 2007: Ch. 10).

Here too there are always likely to be local as well as distant participants in the process with their own interests, preconceptions and variegated agendas in the formulation of data. All this is part of how language is actually used and exploited, so that documentation too is unavoidably an active, creative and far from neutral process.

One long-standing image envisaged the analysis and interpretation of data as naturally belonging to the outsider-investigators. They were the ones capable of synthesizing and expertly studying the matter provided by the insider-informants. But by now many field researchers have moved away from older notions of 'informants' and 'subjects' towards acknowledging the interactive nature of research through such terminologies as 'consultants', 'collaborators', 'co-researchers'. Native scholars and thinkers analyse and organize data, and local metalinguistic conceptualizations – and, no doubt, models of language – shape how the 'data' is presented and synthesized. This complex collaborative process presumably now needs to be recognized rather than hidden. And in the world of today, anyway, who now is insider, who outsider?

As for how and where one finds the data, as an anthropologist I start with an inclination towards participant observation and informal inter-action in addition to local questioning, preferring that to eliciting data outside the field. But having thought further about how verbal and other cultural formulations work in practice, I now recognize that as a somewhat blinkered view. For ultimately all these forms are humanly produced products, and it would be misleading to privilege some as 'counting', others as not.

But equally all data, wherever it originates, has to be treated critically, with full awareness of the providers' social situatedness, whether outside or within 'the field'. Looking for neutral informants channelling neutral data is unrealistic. The data we have are recorded from, assisted by, enacted by, written by, transmuted through people of particular kinds, all with their own preconceptions, characteristics and agenda in terms of, for example, their age, gender, religion, education, politics and much more. And this need not exclude, where they exist, the younger non-fluent or perhaps multilingual speakers. And all are doubtless operating in the context of a developing situation of learning and changing, where the end is unlikely to be the same as the beginning – and a situation furthermore in which the investigators' and sponsors' own position, concerns and policy intentions are all part of the equation.

Not that there is anything reprehensible about this play of interests, diversities or politics. This has always been the background to the practices of translation and of language planning, and to the struggles over what is to count as the same or separate – or original. But the controversies need to be recognized. If certain groups or forms are prioritized on the assumption, for example, that they are the prime bearers of 'the language' – whether the older speakers, the non-schooled, the newer literates, the bilingual children, the travelled, the stay-at-homes – then that decision needs to be manifest. For language documentation can never be – has never been – a matter of detached and objective pebble-gathering, but an intensely human process of selection, analysis and, inevitably, manipulation. And it is in this context that I now find the once simple-sounding and serviceable distinction between data and metadata so much muddier that it seemed at first. As in many other areas of life, there is perhaps never really 'primary' data in some sense of being 'pure', 'traditional', 'authentic'. Rather there are human beings who live in the world and formulate their interventions whether as 'speakers', 'analysts', advocates, politicians – or, more likely, a mixture of all of these and more.

So what ...

The documentation of 'a' language, 'endangered' or other, remains an important and inspiring endeavour. But it is clearly neither simple nor neutral. Like others, no doubt, I continue to puzzle over what can be delimited as 'language', and hence, inevitably, over what can count as 'data' and what would be needed to document a language.

Perhaps these uncertainties are unavoidable. Whatever 'language' is or is not taken to be – written text, performance, abstract system, meaning, action, people deploying resources from across the interpenetrating modes of human communication, or even, by now, an outdated term – there can be no single 'right' or (perhaps) cross-culturally neutral or apolitical view of it. Selective choices are inevitable. But we should be clear that we are making them, that by going down one route we are excluding others, and – finally – that our decisions about what data counts may mean in effect tacitly lining up with some particular position about the nature and working of 'language'.

2

Playing with the heroes of human history

'Orality' and 'literacy' are conventionally the chief protagonists of our epic human story. But as we shall see, this is to overlook the many other modalities which, in some cultures at least, may – perhaps shockingly to Western susceptibilities – for the people concerned take the precedence. The myths of 'literacy' and print which have supported the venture of Western expansion – and in a sense not unreasonably so – now need to be challenged so we can at length reach a more nuanced view of human communication and experience.

'Human history = the history of language'

What makes us human is our possession of language; that has long been the refrain of both popular wisdom and academic exposition. Thus 'language is the specific human character, the essence of our humanity' (Keesing and Strathern 1998: 26), 'the quintessential human attribute' (Pilbeam 1992: 4), 'the fundamental difference between human and animal societies' (Elias 1991: 114), 'the most distinctive single criterion for defining what sets us apart from our closest relatives in the animal world' (James 2003: 142). The 'qualitative leap' between humans and apes came in 'the development of language as a referential, time- and space-transcending sign system' (Luckmann 1995: 176). The same theme is echoed across otherwise diverse disciplines and theoretical perspectives, from general books on communication asserting that 'only with language did we become really human' (Rosengren 1999: 28) or 'when humans crossed the threshold of language … [they] distanced themselves from the rest of creation' (Finch 2003: 1) to Chomsky's insistence on the faculty of language as 'a true "species property"' (2000: 3). Whether it originated in some momentous event, in a wired-in language instinct or inbuilt 'language organ', or through gradual development from more primitive stages, the distinctiveness of humankind, it seems, lies in our possession and practice of language.

This tale of human division from animals through language, repeated and repeated both now and in earlier centuries, is sometimes asserted as a truism, sometimes recounted with an air of originality and profundity, a deep wisdom to be constantly rediscovered. Jack Goody is categorical, seeing a shift 'from gesture to language' as fundamental for the human condition.

> The most significant elements of any human culture are undoubtedly channelled through words, and reside in the particular range of meanings and attitudes which members of any society attach to their verbal symbols. ... Language is the specific human attribute, the critical means of interaction between individuals, the foundation of the development of what we call 'culture' and of the way in which learned behaviour is transmitted from one generation to the next. (Goody 1968: 28, 1987: 3)

For I. A. Richards language is 'the instrument of all our distinctively human development, of everything in which we go beyond the other animals' (1936: 161). Or again, in the resounding words of Thomas Astle, eighteenth-century Keeper of Records at the Tower of London, 'Without speech we should scarcely have been rational beings' (Astle 1784: 2).

The tale is further elaborated to portray the two great forms through which this mark and fulfilment of humanity has been manifested in human history. There is, first of all, speech – oral language. And then came written language. In the language-based story this advent of writing is critical for the unfolding of human history. This theme rings time and time again through the centuries. The fifteenth-century author of one of the earliest European vernacular grammars, Antonio de Nebrija, saw writing as the greatest invention of humankind:

> Among all the things that human beings discovered through experience, or that were shown to us by divine revelation in order to polish and embellish human life, nothing has been more necessary, nor benefited us more, than the invention of letters. (Nebrija 1926 [1492]: 234 Book I, Ch. 2, trans. Mignolo 1994: 95)

Two centuries later Thomas Astle was expressing parallel ideas on writing and human progress:

> The noblest acquisition of mankind is SPEECH, and the most useful art is WRITING. The first, eminently, distinguishes MAN from the brute creation; the second, from uncivilized savages. ... [Writing is] an invention which hath contributed more than all others to the improvement of mankind. (1784: 1, 10)

A century later saw remarkably similar sentiments being enunciated by the anthropologist Edward Burnett Tylor:

> The invention of writing was the greatest movement by which mankind rose from barbarism to civilization. How vast its effect was, may be best measured by looking at the low condition of tribes still living without it, dependent on memory for their traditions and rules of life, and unable to amass knowledge as we do by keeping records of events, and storing up new observations for the use of future generations. (1881: 179)

The tale resounds through more recent years too. For the mid-twentieth-century sociologist Talcott Parsons, writing was a 'watershed' in social evolution, 'the focus of the fateful development out of primitiveness' (1966: 26), while the long-running UNESCO position set writing as the dividing line that separated 'those who master nature, share out the world's riches among themselves, and set out for the stars' from 'those who remain fettered in their inescapable poverty and the darkness of ignorance' (UNESCO 1966: 29): literacy is the 'prerequisite for citizenship and for human and social development' (UNESCO 2001). Jack Goody's strikingly influential publications over nearly half a century have similarly told of 'the transforming effects of literate activity on human life' and its 'primary importance in the history of human cultures' (Goody 2000: 2, 3–4), where the differences between primitive and advanced cultures are attributable to the advent of writing and writing underpins civilization (Goody 1987: 291, 300). 'The emergence of writing and literate activity some five thousand years ago transformed human life', he writes, 'a quantum jump in human consciousness, in cognitive awareness' (Goody 2000: blurb, 1998: 1).

These accounts, far-reaching and emotive, correlate the ideologies and technologies of language with modernity and the mission of the West. They feed on that same familiar paradigm of the powerful binary oppositions that divide humankind and demarcate the great eras of its history: orality versus literacy, primitive versus civilized.

The linguistically driven narrative has been so pervasively and consistently deployed that it might indeed be described as a foundational myth of the West. Like other myths that set out the nature and destiny of humankind, it is no doubt differentially believed, at times contested (some contrary voices are considered below) and certainly turned to many different purposes. But it indubitably presents a profoundly evocative and compelling account. Europe fulfils the foreordained human destiny through its attainment of writing, and above all of print, buttressed by the successes of modernizing science and rationality to which this led. Human history is to be read through the glass of language and its technologies.

A more complicated story

The language-centred story is told and retold, overtly a descriptive and incontrovertible account articulating shared assumptions about the nature and destiny of humankind. But it is a tendentious one all the same. It projects a tale of language and alphabetic literacy moving humanity onward into the scientific and democratic regimes of the West. The actions and structures of the West over the centuries of expansion nestle well within this encompassing tale, mutually intertwined with the social arrangements and ideologies of education, socialization, science, expansion, empire, social mobility, modernity … Language, not least in the extensive projects of biblical translation, was a primary vehicle in the missionary conversion process and crucial for the civilizing vision of the West: Simon Gikandi well notes 'the central role accorded literary texts in the project of colonial modernity by both the colonizer and the colonized' (2004: 385). Language and writing fed into and out of the power structures with 'language [as] the means of the spiritual subjugation', as Ngugi wa Thiong'o famously had it. The alphabetic script – 'universally employed by civilized peoples' (Diringer 1968, vol. 1: 13) – was the 'ultimate tool of conquest' (Griffiths 1997: 144).

The linguistic myth of human history, for all it looks universal, is no neutral account. The essence of human-ness is posited as language; and language in its two predestined modes, first oral then written, as unrolling the stages of human history. The tale echoes that Enlightenment ideology in which language, and especially written language, is the condition of rationality, civilization and progress, attaining its apotheosis in the alphabetic writing of the West. Music, dance and drama fall out of the picture. So do the gestural, pictorial, sculptural, sonic, tactile, bodily, affective and artefactual dimensions of human life. What we have is a cognitive language-centred model of the nature and destiny of humanity.

Over the last centuries this account has without doubt inspired and authorized many previous actions, experiences and understandings. But it is not inevitably subscribed to in all traditions or times, nor does it necessarily provide a trusty cross-cultural guide. It is not only the 1960s Limba who, for all their interest in language, might resist the notion that verbal language is self-evidently the distinctive and leading human attribute. Many others would now query the once-unquestioned practice, sanctioned by that same myth, of translating multisensory African performances into thin textual lines and, as Steve Chimombo well points out, classifications of African art that prioritize 'the verbal, exclude other art forms (e.g. the visual) which are inextricably interrelated with all the rest' (Chimombo 1988: 2). The linguistic focus may indeed chime well with certain aspects of Western history, but is less felicitous for illuminating other dimensions of human cultural experience and scarcely a universal or comprehensive account of human destiny.

The tale has indeed functioned as a kind of mythical charter, enunciating and validating a Western vision and at the same time projecting an image of 'Africa' as, in its essence, 'oral', 'pre-literate' and (by that very lack of writing) not fully civilized. It is over-simple however just to castigate it as the self-interested Western tale. 'The West', after all, is scarcely monolithic in its geography, history or varied social experiences, and there have been recurring alternative themes too.

The powerful Lockean version, for example, in which language is rational, referential, decontextualized, the key to scientific progress, is countered in the tradition of Herder and his followers, where the emphasis on language is complemented by an interest in the role of feeling and imagination and the scope for intertextuality, context and sensory celebration (see especially Bauman and Briggs 2000, 2003, Briggs 2002). And it was Western writers, after all, like Bakhtin (1968) and Huizinga (1949) who highlighted the realities of carnival and of play, and the philosopher R. G. Collingwood who emphasized non-verbal communicative modes like bodily gesture, dance and music (1938: 242 and Ch. 11 *passim*).

The present seems to be one of those periods when alternative perspectives to the (still prevalent) linguistic myth are becoming more visible. They are articulated not just in the by now commonplace critiques of ethnocentric grand narrative, but across many disciplines and backgrounds. The practices of language are coming to be recognized as processes for empirical study rather than primarily as uplifting tokens of human destiny or prescriptive ideals; so too, if as yet less prominently, are the ideologies surrounding language. Current moves in cultural history, sociology, material culture and studies of 'the body' are between them undermining the assumed centrality of the word to human life; indeed, it has been proposed that a 'sensual revolution' is now supplanting the so-called linguistic turn in the human sciences (Howes 2005: 1). In anthropology (though not just there) there has been a flowering of studies of sensual forms: 'of the visual, of art, of aesthetics; of "performance", of body language; and of the aural – the interpretation of sound, of music and song' (James 2003: 74). The resulting appreciation of the multiple modes of human life – touches, sounds, sights, smells, movements, material artefacts – and of shared experiences, dynamic interactions and bodily engagements at once takes us beyond the purely verbal and cognitive and uncovers the partiality of the narrow linguistic tale.

The challenge is also coming through our changing communication technologies. It has to be said, of course, that their 'impact' has often been much exaggerated, seriously over-simplifying the complexity of human action and of cultural and political controls and ideologies. And in any case, 'new' communication media long precede the present generation. But with all the caveats, recent technological developments may indeed be playing some part in cajoling our sensibilities to realities beyond (spoken and written) words.

The technology of writing and the practices of enscription privilege the substantiality of written words. It was these, whether composed on the page or transcribed from performance, that once seemed to give the 'real thing': the durable and materialized text. But audio technology has enabled attention to realities missed by pen-and-paper recording. Parry and Lord's phonograph revealed variability and challenged the assumption of abiding verbal texts (Lord 1960), just as audio recordings have uncovered acoustic subtleties in African oral genres and opened our ears to once-unappreciated facets of performance.

Audio is part of popular usage and perception too. In Africa as elsewhere people employ audio technologies for their own purposes: composing, performing, listening, and more. Radio has long been a medium for dissemination and publication, from story, song and performed poetry to oratory, plays and talk shows (Fardon and Furniss 2000, Spitulnik 2004), and for years now tape and cassette recorders have been readily used devices for composition and recordings; decades ago they were already a regular part of Somali camel-riders' gear as they criss-crossed the desert. Cassettes of Haya epics are on sale from street vendors in Tanzania (Mbele 2004: 105), dub poetry grew from the complex intermixture of creative poetic composition with sound recording technology, and recordings on disc or web are a regular part of the popular culture scene.

These extralinguistic elements, often lost in the transmission of orality into literacy, can again be recaptured through technology. The reaction of the audience, the performer's intonation, voice quality and emphasis, the effects of rhythm, context and the speed of performance are lost in the written version, but can once again come alive in the technologized version (Kaschula 2003: 8–9).

Audio technologies enable us not only to hear but to document and embody music, volume, tempo, sonic structures, dynamics, intonation or intensity, and multiple ensembles as well as solo performers, and bring to notice elements that had before been defined out of existence by the prioritizing of the verbal.

The visual is being more clearly revealed too. Certain visual dimension have, of course, long been capturable in still images such as the illuminating photographs of Tuareg and Xhosa narrative performances (Calame-Griaule 1985, Scheub 1997a, Scheub and Zenani 1992). But it is the moving-image technologies that have truly enlarged our awareness. They can make real the sequential deployment of gesture, display, material symbols, spacing and dance, supplementing still photography by encapturing movement, dynamic development and the seen dialectics of audience and performer interactions. They do so, furthermore, in temporal flow with a sense of immediacy and personality – a counter both to the single-voice text and to the anonymous 'tradition' sometimes purveyed through more distanced written representations.

In Africa as elsewhere people are now well acquainted with the realities of moving images in television, film and video, and of how performers can disseminate their creations more widely than in the immediate moment and place of live performance. Christian video narratives interfused with 'indigenous imaginations' circulate in Nigeria (Obododimma 2001), a Yoruba popular theatre group performs on television and video as well as on tour (Barber 2000), video technologies are familiarly drawn on in a host of contexts to capture the realities of performance and experience, and film is an established form in and about Africa which is turned to many purposes (both 'research' and other). With all their well-known problems of cost or unequal access, the enlarged perspective of video technologies has unquestionably given new insight not just into some secondary dimension at the margin but into the solidity of the visual acts and arts of performance.

The multimedia opportunities increasingly (if unequally) offered by computers have further extended the narrower focus on words. CD-ROMs and web displays, with their facility for the vivid multimedia combinations of colour, shape, movement, image, graphic and sound interlaced with individual creativity and playful dynamics, can move between, around and beyond oral/written boundaries, presenting multiplex performance modes in both real and transferred time. Such resources are now exploited not just by scholars or activists but by African artists and their admirers: performances by the Xhosa praise poet Zolani Mkiva, for example, are available for a worldwide audience on the web (www.makingmusic.co.za – Kaschula 2003: 2). Such media give a new kind of reality to dimensions that once seemed (at best) peripheral to the firm centrality of print.

The 'new' technologies have their limitations. They may have marvellously alerted us to aural, visual and moving elements but leave other dimensions uncaptured (smell, touch, bodily presence); nor, as Tedlock well points out for earlier technologies, do they automatically and immediately affect people's sense of reality (Tedlock 1985: 341). Nevertheless they are taking us beyond one-line verbalized text to greater awareness of co-creators, multiple voices and multiple media, giving substance to dimensions screened out in the technology of writing – to realities that could before too easily be presumed to be either, on the one hand, merely ephemeral and tangential or, on the other, only truly existent when translated into verbal text. A recent international conference of the Society for Oral Literature in Africa (held in Banjul 2004) is symptomatic of this newer perspective, embracing as it did such topics as music, theatre, dance, textile oracy, contemporary song, audio, video, film, radio, hypermedia and multimedia archiving. The take on what oral forms 'are' is being stretched from writable one-voice texts into the multifacetedness of multimodal enactment.

From this angle, too, the once apparently clear concepts of orality and literacy – of speech and writing – have become cloudier. Speech may have been pictured as the essential human attribute, but it does not stand on its own: it is inextricably intertwined with other modes of human interaction, gestural, bodily, visual, artefactual, tactile.

Nor are the echoes and overtones of either performance or text purely verbal. Proverbs are not just spoken and written but drummed, carved, miniaturized in gold weights, or represented in figurines, masks and cloth, carrying multimodal evocations whatever their immediate medium. Verbal language is both complemented and interpenetrated by multisensory products and practices – by the great textile arts of Africa, so notable for their range of graphic and figurative expression, by representations in wood or beadwork, by music and dance, no less than by the more recent arts of film, video and electronic communication, between them both eroding and extending the ostensibly comprehensive categories of oral and written.

The image of some single (West-generated) 'writing' ushering in the second act of the great human drama has also been muddied by our gathering appreciation of the diverse forms of literacy. Not all writing systems are alphabetic, nor can they necessarily be analysed as merely the transparent transliteration of spoken language – of language pure and simple. Pictorial and decorative dimensions can play a prominent role and even the familiar alphabetic scripts are not made up just of words but also of such other – integral – elements as layout, space, colour, shape or texture. And it is not just in form but also in practice that 'literacy' varies, for people use writing and reading in a multiplicity of ways and through a huge diversity of systems, situations and social arrangements – not so much literacy as multiliteracies. The once-hard concept of 'writing' has turned into something more fluid and unstable: manifest in diverse shapes and deployments and, with the contemporary development of 'soft' text and visual display, itself often both multimodal and evanescent. 'Language as oral' and 'language as written' no longer look clearly distinct from each other in attributes or usages, nor to be the only players in the destiny of humankind.

The linguistic myth has not gone away, intertwined as it is with powerfully entrenched social institutions. But there is now perhaps a greater inclination across a series of social and humanistic disciplines to draw away from the assumption that the way to pin down reality in durable form must naturally be through language. This in turn is to question the presupposition, perhaps held above all by intellectuals, that only verbally captured elements truly exist and are worthy of academic study. The challenges now coming from many different directions, not least in people's lived practices, are unveiling the multiple dimensions and diversities screened out in the account that accords the central role to language and its two epiphanies in orality and literacy. The tale of humanity goes beyond the verbal, and to focus on the fortunes of language is to leave out a vast proportion of human reality.

Words in their place

That is not to say there is no place for words and language; if nothing else, the contents of this volume tell otherwise. My point is rather that getting rid of the over-ambitious claims for 'language' in fact allows a clearer perspective on humans' active use of words – but words now seen, more modestly, as set in the context of, and intermingled with, the array of other communicative modes of which verbal language is only one.

And it *is* still a wonderful mode. The nodes of human cultural production in which the verbal in some sense plays a prominent role – from Greek or Japanese drama, European medieval song or epic narrative to personal life stories, praise poetry, rap or popular song on the web – are indeed among the stupendous achievements of humankind. Throughout the world and the centuries, human creations in verbalized narrative, in poetic performance, in all the many forms of oral engagement touched on in this volume and elsewhere are not just for some limited utilitarian purpose – though they can include that – but among the central realities and glories of human living. English-language terms like 'poetry', 'story', 'literature', or indeed 'orature' or 'oraurality', may be culture-bound indeed, but for all their limitations they alert us to a continuing and striking dimension of human activity.

Just what is covered by those loosely linked terms 'language', 'words', 'the verbal' admittedly continues to be elusive, more so than may seem implied throughout this volume (or, indeed, in most analyses of human cultural activity). Defining 'language' may look a relatively neutral process of pinning down something with some kind of autonomous existence, an assumption that chimes well with the linguistic tale. Some recent accounts would argue, however, that the notion of 'language' is in fact irretrievably rooted in particular social and historical phases and ideologies; not, after all, 'an object that exists prior to and independently of efforts to study it' (Briggs 2002: 493). Amid such debates I am not aspiring to carve out some precise demarcation for this inescapably complex and loaded term, but I do need to return briefly to the issues about boundaries raised both at the start and by the further discussion and topics throughout the volume.

The growing interest in context and dialogic interaction that has increasingly emerged over recent decades is challenging the narrower model of languge as single-voiced, abstract and referential. The boundaries have become more fuzzy, if only because of the shift of gaze onto the complicated and diverse ways people act and interact, where the verbal dimension becomes more verb or adverb than demarcatable noun. The current emphasis on the multisensory has led in the same direction, with the further suggestion that multimodality may be not a secondary feature of language but central to its usage. Speech includes, at the least, non-verbal acoustic elements like volume, intensity, speed, timbre, emphasis, intonation, pacing, sequence, length, cadence, together perhaps with laughter, shrieks, sighs, hesitations, silence ... the multidimensionality of oral expression has been a constant theme of this volume, as of other recent writing. Written formulations too are shot through with non-verbal features, predominantly visual (space, layout, picture, colour, texture, shading, graphics), but also sometimes tactual and auditory too. Non-verbal elements brushed aside in traditional grammars and dictionaries by the focus on words and their grammatical and syntactical interrelations are arguably now receiving more attention, instanced in the 1994 *Encyclopedia of Language and Linguistics*' conclusion that 'the central element of [language] is verbal but [it] contains as an essential component a substantial non-verbal element, e.g. intonation, stress, punctuation, etc.'(Asher and Simpson 1994, vol. 10: 5137 [Glossary entry for 'language'])

In this larger view of language which extends it beyond the restricted bounds of dictionary-defined writable words, the question of just where the frontiers are to be set becomes a culturally variable and far from self-evident matter. Where 'language' ends and 'music' begins is a moot point for example, perhaps differently construed in different traditions. There is the question of gesture too, in standard definitions often set apart from language, but recent studies of the intimate ways it is systematically coordinated with speech have led some to urge that the boundaries of language should perhaps be widened to encompass this visual, dynamic and embodied mode of communicating. The broader perspectives on 'language' bring out its intrinsically multidimensional and culturally diverse features.

A contrasting but ultimately complementary approach is to retain a relatively narrow demarcation of language – but with two provisos. First, it is not a matter of some separate entity or activity but a somewhat vague, overlapping and ragged-at-the-edges sector within the multifarious constellation of human arts and activities. Whatever boundaries we suggest are unlikely to be either stable or cross-culturally neutral (even 'words', those apparently hard entities, do not everywhere have the same independent and delimited existence that can seem self-evident to those socialized into recent alphabetic traditions). Second, since a full account of language must surely include looking at both usage and context, we have to bring into the picture the other modes and media with which it is in practice variously intermingled. From this perspective, language is only one of several communicative-expressive modes: it works together with them and cannot be properly understood alone.

Whether we take the wider or the narrower delineation, we need to go beyond just words. Language has to be envisaged as either, on the one hand, made up of more than just spoken and written words, or, on the other, as one mode among many, working in multimodal settings where the verbal element may or may not play the primary role. Either way this leads to a more questioning approach to language than in the apparently unproblematic linguistic myth, relating it not to prescribed ideal forms or single cultural-linguistic traditions, but to actual human practices and their diverse settings.

Parallel dilemmas face us in delineating terms like 'oral texts', 'oral literature', 'oral performance', or more general concepts like 'orality' or 'orature'. One strategy, consonant with the larger picture of language, is to define the 'oral' as itself multimodal, essentially broader and more multiple than just the 'verbal'. The alternative is to use the term 'oral' (and its composites) as just one of many modes – not as clearly delimited as it once seemed, admittedly, nor to be understood in isolation, but as a roughly recognizable, if fuzzy, sector to do with the vocalized and (in some vague sense) verbal dimensions within the overlapping fields of human arts and communication. I suspect that, like some other authors, I am wavering between these two perspectives on the 'oral' – the broader and the narrower – perhaps at times simultaneously drawing on both, but have probably mostly presupposed the second, somewhat narrower sense. This arguably has advantages for certain purposes, to be pursued in a moment. But let me first re-emphasize that it has to go along with a recognition that the term is indeed problematic and to an extent culture-bound, its delimitation and interrelationships inescapably ragged. The ideas of 'oral', 'orality' etc. need to be used with some modesty rather than taken for granted as transparent and independent concepts, far less with the unquestioned priority in human affairs projected in the grand linguistic myth. Equally important, a proper understanding of the actual practice of human communication and expression, both 'artistic' and 'ordinary', must include setting words in the context of the other modes and media used alongside them. Often enough it is a matter of interpenetrating and inextricably interwoven dimensions in which the verbal is just one – and not necessarily, in any given situation or genre, the most salient.

Looking at language as only one among several dimensions goes some way towards putting words in their place. It pushes us towards recognizing the full range of modes present in any given case rather than taking for granted – the temptation intellectuals can so readily fall into – that the crucial element is verbal. It still needs saying that, as Okpewho well put it of oral performance in Africa, 'the words spoken are only part of a general spectacle designed to please the ears and the eyes' (Okpewho 1992: 48); that African, Caribbean and African American drama is characterized by 'the interdependence of music/dance/gesture to language' (Morales 2003: 151); or, even more pertinently since it is applied to one very specific genre, that Kpelle epic performances from Liberia involve the intermingling of singing, narration, dramatic enactment and instrumental accompaniment, with 'sounds and movements textured with the voice ... an aural type of texture augmented with dramatic gestures ... The epic is heard, seen and felt' (Stone 1998: 135, 137).

Differentiating the verbal – and in this sense the oral – for analytic purposes, however roughly, can alert us both to the combinations of modes in any given instance and to the ideologies and social arrangements that may lie behind them. The pre-eminence conceptually accorded to the verbally textualized in (much) Western tradition does not automatically apply everywhere, and dimensions recognized in one set of conventions as irretrievably coming together in particular genres may not do so in others, or may be prioritized or conceptualized differently. As David Coplan points out in a plea that applies more widely than just to Basotho migrants' songs:

> My preferred] term 'auriture' ... makes no claim for the universality of intersense modalities in African performance but rather insists that empirical ethnoaesthetic categories be investigated rather than assumed. (1994: 8–9).

Finally then, we must recognize the diverse ways that such 'intersense modalities' are used in and by different genres, traditions, occasions, interested parties, registers and linguistic practices. The verbal element may or may not play a leading part. At any rate, its centrality is a question to be investigated rather than a conclusion to be taken for granted.

3

'Artisting the self':
A tale of personal story

Is life a story? Jerome Bruner, first among equals, teaches us that we construct ourselves and our experience through the arts of story. This approach is here exemplified from a series of first-hand cases from urban Britain (some dramatic experiences too!) analysed in relation to narrative theory and studies of personal identity.

Strikingly the tellers presented here had never, as we shall see, told their life stories in a sustained form before. And yet they all somehow already had the artistry and structure needed for their (orally) narrated life stories. These had, it seemed, a literary structure too (though how far the term 'oral literature' is a viable one and what it might mean must be left to a later chapter), well acquainted in practice if not in theory with the concepts of theme, motif and narrative structure.

One woman's tale

Let me plunge straight in by quoting some story-tellers from the new town of Milton Keynes, recorded on cassette in their homes in the 1990s.

First then, Shirley Lambert.[1] She was then in her early thirties, living in a council house in Milton Keynes. She talks about her life.

Our family personally, we had a lot of trouble with our family because we had a violent father, and my mother was actually mentally ill. We didn't do well at school at all because we had so much trouble with the family, it was more had we survived the day, you know, than actual getting down to it. My father would wake us up at three o'clock in the morning because there was dust on the stairs, so we would all have to

---

1 This and the other names here are pseudonymns: though the tellers were happy for their tales to be known, they almost (not quite) all preferred not to publicize their individual names.

sweep the whole house, you know what I mean, and so you didn't get a lot of sleep and then by the time you got to school you felt too tired and things like this and we didn't learn a lot. My teacher just thought I was disruptive and I ended up going into a children's home.

I had actually left home by the time I went in the children's home, because it was a residential place in Aylesbury, what we did was come home for the weekends, but I had actually been kicked out of home, so they didn't realize that I wasn't going home. So what we would do was, we would go to the children's home during the week, come home and just walk the streets for the whole weekend. There was a lot to walk, and because there were fields and things like that you could hide in Milton Keynes then quite easily. And then when my assessment was over we actually went to college and everything, they decided that yes, you can now go back to your family, but what they didn't know was I couldn't go back to the family, because everything was like through the courts, and as soon as I walked in the door and all the abuse would start up again, the fighting, so coming up to fourteen I left home, and I actually lived with a lady who I looked after her children, and that was the only home life I knew.

Job-wise it was very difficult because I was so young I couldn't get a job in Milton Keynes, I couldn't claim, because I didn't have the sense to claim, you know for help, I knew I was far too young, so I didn't even go and check out or try and bang on anybody's door to beg for it, you know, so you just made do, you know.

When I was about fifteen I got a small job in a little clothes store, but I got in awful trouble there because it is like all that glitters is gold to me, and because I had worked there for a pittance and couldn't have the things that were in the store I decided to help myself! And that was that, and I remember that was my first ever job and looking back now I think to myself if only I had the sense to not see everything as glittering and you can just do that, it would have been quite good, it would have been a good memory but it is a bad memory for me to know that I had messed it up quite horribly.

After that, coming up sixteen round here was quite fun. Sixteen/ seventeen I worked for McDonalds until I was about nineteen, but it was great I was earning money, them days you could get a flat if you were earning money, I got a little flat and everything and I was on like sky-high, this is brilliant you know my life is coming together and I used to earn money ... and thought this was all great you can buy a pair of shoes every two months, this is brilliant, this was the time when platforms were in, and I was wearing flats, you know.

That went very well, by this time I had lost contact with my family because I couldn't go back to the house, and with all the turmoil it was easier not going back, because then I would have to think about the family and try and get my life together, and I couldn't manage the two, so up till I was about eighteen, I didn't have much contact since I left with the family, and then I went back. One day I saw my little sisters outside a shop, and they were terrified of me, and I couldn't get why they were terrified of me, and I thought oh talk to me, and they said we are not allowed to talk to you, and you have got to go because their father was in the shop, and I said this is ridiculous you know, I thought what is happening, and so it was apparently he had left my mother, and taken all the kids and furniture and left her in the house with nothing, you know. So we didn't have much furniture to start off with, but he took things like the cooker, so what is she heating on, you know, took the fridge and everything, and in the conversation they kind of told me she was ill.

So me, worry, worry, worry, backed up courage and a couple of friends and we went down there, and she actually had turned mad, and she was like living off cat food and things like that, you know, in big Milton Keynes, nobody realized, no neighbours realized, how awful it was, and actually I had to commit her at eighteen to the mental hospital.

She continues with her story: how she helped her sisters, coped with other hard experiences, continued to 'back up courage', and started to feel established in the local community. She concludes:

Everybody is allowed a chance, and I didn't have the chance and I gave myself the chance though and I think if I can do it anybody can.

I mean like I said ending the story, I went all to the ripe age of fourteen like and I couldn't even spell my own name, and I had to learn, and now like I'm the most magazine queen now, it is like I am always reading, and anybody can do it. I might not be a professional, I can't do a degree, my concentration span right doesn't, you know I can't sit still that long, I couldn't do something like that. But then you can always do something else, I can be special somewhere else, and that is basically my life.

When we read a personal narrative of this kind we are, it seems, brought face to face with the most personal point in the circuit of our culture: individual experience. With art too, it seems, both verbal and performed. And, it would seem, with something literary too (the fraught term 'oral literature' might or might not seem appropriate here, an issue to be tackled in a later chapter).

The nature of this 'individual experience' turns out to be rather more complex, however, than it seems at first sight. But it should be clear at least that in focusing on personal stories in this chapter, we are in some sense moving down from the level of formal structure, mass media or large-scale institutions and industries, to that of the everyday lives of ordinary individuals as they formulate it in their own words.

The story here (abridged as it is) raises the issue of personal identity. 'Who am I?' was a question which, in one sense, Shirley Lambert's narrative was itself grappling with. It is indeed a serious one, which all readers will no doubt have considered at various points in their lives. Indeed one common response could simply be to start telling the story of your life.

The idea of 'self as story' both overlaps and also partly contrasts with other models of identity. It also extends the idea of 'culture' and 'media' beyond the organizational structures of, say, the cultural industries, broadcasting or the published media into the more informal level of the everyday modes through which we express ourselves in personal terms, telling our own stories. In doing so it thus follows the same assumption as in the last chapter: that it can be valuable to look not just to the products of the professionals and specialists but also, as emphasized ealier, to the practices and experiences of ordinary people in the setting of everyday life.

This chapter thus starts by setting the currently popular concept of 'story' in a more general perspective through the discussion of some recent work on narrative. It then moves on to explaining a view of the self as essentially 'storied' – constructed and experienced through self-narratives. This is a view expressed in the work of, among others, Jerome Bruner. Both in the examples of personal stories at the everyday level and the more general discussion, you will find that personal stories are being analysed less as the reflection of some irreducible 'inner experience' or 'external reality' (outside culture, as it were) than as both culturally constructed and actively en-storied by their tellers. In this story-based view of the self, the individual story-tellers are viewed as at once drawing on narrative conventions – a kind of art form as it were – to realize their stories of the self and themselves as creative and artistic actors in the production of culture and identity.

Humanity, narrative

One response, then, to the question of 'Who are you?' might simply be to tell a story of your life.

This may seem a trivial reply to a serious matter. It looks simplistic and 'merely' personal when stated just like that. Certainly it seems at first sight to have little of the grandeur of other ways of theorizing the self: in terms, say, of Freudian or Foucauldian theory or of sociological approaches which illuminate the complex social factors and interactions which can influence – arguably determine – our lives in a whole range of previously unappreciated ways.

But the concept of 'story' or 'narrative' is becoming another recognized approach to identity. It links too to an increasing stress by some scholars on the profound significance of narrative in the shaping and interpretation of human culture more generally. With all the controversies that such an approach involves, it has nonetheless emerged as a powerful tool for the analysis of cultural products and processes.

Given its current influence, let me start with a short diversion to give some background to this general idea of narrative, before moving on to specific cases (if you prefer to look at the personal narratives first, you can return to this section later). Despite the many controversies involved in studying narrative, one essential theme recurs again and again. This is – to put it at its simplest – a basic view that human beings are story-telling animals. Whether explicitly or silently, we join together and make sense of our experiences in a more, or less, coherent narrative.

> Children, only animals live entirely in the Here and Now. Only nature knows neither memory nor history. But man – let me offer you a definition – is the story-telling animal. Wherever he goes he wants to leave behind not a chaotic wake, not an empty space, but the comforting marker-buoys and trail-signs of stories. He has to go on telling stories. He has to keep on making them up. (Swift 1983: 53–4)

That quotation from Graham Swift's *Waterland* is in deliberately simplified language. But (provided you can bypass the distraction of what some would regard as sexist terminology) he is aptly summarizing what has become a central theme in recent analysis.

There are also, to take a (superficially) very different matter, 'narratives of corporate culture and of enterprise', and the memorable – and effective – role of the 'epic tale' of the manager as hero. Here the management consultants are 'story tellers to senior managers' and 'the success of the Corporate Culture narratives may lie in the heroic status attributed to senior managers'. Similarly, 'The company has explicit values and beliefs which its employees share. It has heroes. It has storytellers and stories' (Deal and Kennedy 1989: 12). One formative element in the culture of production, it emerges, is the process by which both managers and employees construct reality by 'telling stories'.

This concept of story is being increasingly applied to people's definitions of reality. In the context of analysing cultural processes, it illuminates how people's ideologies and theories – even if implicit rather than consciously stated – are all the more influential and evocative when they chime with familiar narrative motifs, themes and hero figures.

But it is not just the 'subjects' of academic study who recount stories. Academics and intellectuals too tell their own tales. The grand paradigms of social science, for example, have been described as forms of narrative – the 'good story' told by Marx, Durkheim, Weber or Simmel (Clegg 1993: 15), for instance. Similarly the many interpretations posited within sociology are nowadays often referred to as 'stories'. Indeed this has become one of the dominant themes in cultural studies, where 'narratives and their interwoven textures are the stuff of life' (Inglis 1993: 244). Historians' accounts too, it has been pointed out, are stories about what happened. The term can be applied not just to their straight chronological narratives but also to their varying assumptions about the causes or results of lengthy processes over time. Some of their accounts, for example, are rooted in stories highlighting

the deeds of individual actors, others in very different stories depicting
(for example) class-based causes, revolutionary changes or evolution from
(say) 'traditional' to 'modern' or to 'post-modern' epochs (White 1973,
Cronon 1992). The same 'story' theme is evident in some geography and in
psychology, well illustrated in Sarbin's *Narrative Psychology: The Storied
Nature of Human Conduct* (1986), and of course in the significant role of
story in Freudian therapy. Even the natural sciences are no exception, illustrated in the description of the 'narratives of human evolution' as versions
of the widespread hero tale (Landau 1991).

This usage of 'story' is by now pretty much taken for granted as an
analytic term across a wide range of social science and humanistic disciplines (for further examples, see Plummer 1996: 181 and *passim*). Indeed,
whether due to the influence of sceptical postmodernist critiques or just an
increasing interest in narrative, it seems to have become a widely accepted
convention in much social scientific writing to refer to academic theories
and interpretations as 'stories'.

But just what is implied by these uses of the term 'story' in such contexts?
What difference does such a label make?

It has to be admitted that precisely what is meant by calling something
a 'story' is not always totally clear and there are actually quite a variety
of implications here, differently weighted by different writers. Sometimes
'story' seems to be more a bit of fashionable terminology than a thought-
out analytic term! Or it may be used as just a decorative, if somewhat
faded metaphor. But where the term is applied in a more considered way,
its minimum features are reasonably agreed. Referring to something as a
'story' (or 'narrative' – the two terms will be used synonymously for present
purposes) normally conveys both some idea of time or sequence and an
element of explanation or coherence – some kind of plot that makes sense
to the teller and/or audience. If you look back you can see both of these
in even the sketchy extracts from Shirley Lambert's story. Further, a story
usually manifests a series of accepted conventions about form and content.
In other words, it constitutes a culturally recognized genre.[2]

Applying the term 'story' to either academic interpretations or (insofar
as this is different) to the assumptions of the actors themselves thus implies
that these can be treated as stories. That is, we can analyse them in terms
of their temporal/sequential framework, intelligible plot, and culturally
constructed conventions about what makes up an accepted piece of story-
telling. Certain kinds of protagonists may be expected: the hero for example
– as in the tales of Corporate Culture – or the victim, villain or trickster.
There are likely to be recurrent recognizable plots too. Among these may
be the hero going on a quest; the success or otherwise of evil; a change over

---

2   Further discussion of the complex definitional and related issues can be found in Bauman
1986, Linde 1993, Mumby 1993, Plummer 1996, Prince 1989, Riessman 1993, Rosenwald
and Ochberg 1992.

time from deprivation/suffering/immaturity to riches/happiness/maturity, or from modernity to postmodernity; or, alternatively, the fall from grace from the Golden Age of true community and harmony to the woes of the present – to mention just a few that are widely current in our culture.

One common implication here is that, as summed up in Graham Swift's view of human beings as essentially 'story-telling animals', a narrative framework is a characteristically human way for formulating and conveying experience. As Barbara Hardy put it:

> We dream in narrative, day-dream in narrative, remember, anticipate, hope, despair, believe, doubt, plan, revise, criticize, construct, gossip, learn, hate and love by narrative. (1968: 5)

Equally relevant is the implication that insofar as they are labelled 'stories', such formulations can be analysed less as simple reflections of 'reality' than as texts mediated through the culturally constructed conventions by which they are shaped and told.

For some analysts, applying the concept of 'story' to academic interpretations has yet a further implication. It gives a vantage point on academic writing, enabling a critique of its culturally recognized conventions. In this view, rather than being 'objective', 'neutral' or 'scientific' accounts of reality, academic theories too have their own 'rhetoric' and 'poetics': 'art' as much as 'science'. They are shaped by current narrative conventions in just the same way as the texts of other stories (e.g. Clifford and Marcus 1986, Van Maanen 1988). Non-written texts can be treated similarly. It becomes possible to analyse the 'poetics' of the story conveyed in a particular juxtaposition of photographs, or constructed in an exhibition. The ideas of 'poetics' and of 'story' hint that what is constructed is actually more akin to fiction or poetry, art-fully crafted, than to the disinterested and neutral recording of reality once assumed as the model for academic and scientific enquiry.

Sometimes the label 'story' additionally implies the more extreme claim that the theories put forward by the academics are no more authoritative than stories told in any other voices. Far from being the final word, the interpretations of the scholars – themselves often in a position of power – should not in this view be taken as the authoritative and 'above-the-battle' account. Above all, this argument might go on, the academics' versions should not obscure the definitions of reality in the stories of those they study: the colonized, the 'hidden', the minority groups or, indeed, anyone that 'research' is conducted on, the subjects of the scholars' story-making.

That final position of pointing out that there is a multiplicity of voices, not just those of the dominant scholars, can appropriately lead us back to the central focus of this chapter: the voices of ordinary people speaking about their lives in the context of their everyday activities. So let us now return to personal narratives, moving away from the more theoretical contexts in which the term 'story' is sometimes used (referring for example to the great 'metanarratives' of sociological theory) to the everyday level of the stories of individual tellers about their own lives and experiences.

Stories as the individual voice of the self – or not? First, personal narratives. For if we want to know about people's experience and how they interpret it, there is something to be said for looking not to academics' generalizations but to the stories of the participants themselves. Better still, to stories told not in others' words but as the tellers themselves express them.

For example, we can certainly read informative general accounts of the Industrial Revolution. But how much more vivid an insight we get from a narration of how this was actually experienced in an individual case. Take the case of Thomas Wood's life, to be found in Burnett's fascinating collection of previously unpublished autobiographies, *Useful Toil: Autobiographies of Working People from the 1820s to the 1920s* (1974: 304–12).

Thomas Wood was born in Yorkshire in 1822, the son of a handloom weaver. He started at the local woollen mill at the age of eight, working the regular hours of 6.00 a.m. to 7.30 p.m. But he longed to be delivered from what he called 'the bondage of factory life', and at fourteen managed to persuade his parents to apprentice him to a local 'mechanic' (engineer) manufacturing powerlooms.

> So I was to be a mechanic and have my heart's desire. As will be seen my parents paid dearly for it. Our food was of the plainest, the quantity seldom sufficient. I seldom satisfied my appetite unless I called at Aunt Nancy's after dinner to pick up what she had to spare. As to the luxury of pocket money, it was unknown. ...
>
> There was a [Mechanics'] Institute at Wilsden, perhaps the best in the country then. It was only three miles off, so I resolved to enter that. ... The terms were 1 1/2d. per week ... more than I could raise. I therefore got bundles of rotten sticks in the wood and sold them for firewood. Turnip-tops and nettles when in season with mushrooms I collected, and whatever would sell. Well pleased was I when I had 3d. to meet my fortnight's contributions. Then, as to reading, in winter I had to read by firelight excepting when I could afford a 1/2d. candle, which I used to save to read with in bed. I have read perhaps scores of times till 12 or 1 o'clock. There were no curtains to fire. There were no interruptions. A house with seven or eight children on one floor is a fine opportunity for the display of patience on the part of a student or an earnest reader. Get into bed for the warmth and then the luxury of an unbroken reading was a treat that compensated for any privations, and lifted me, for the time being, into another world ... (Burnett 1974: 307–8)

Autobiographical accounts of this kind perhaps once seemed too 'trivial' or, alternatively, too 'personal' for serious academic study. They comprised neither the products of elite writers nor fitted with the 'collective' emphasis typical in (some forms of) social science. But there is now greater interest in such personal accounts. Besides the increasing preoccupation with the idea of 'story/narrative' in general terms, as described in the last section, historians and others now make a point of collecting and analysing working-class autobiographies (for example Burnett 1974, 1982, Vincent 1981; and those of women as well as of men, see e.g. Stanley 1984, 1992, Personal Narratives Group 1989). This trend has been further supported by recent interests in 'history from below' and the turn towards social rather than just political history.

An interest in the life stories of 'ordinary' people has for long been one strand in the social sciences, although often rather submerged compared to more generalized or macro studies. But a specific focus on personal lives has been emerging strongly in recent years (for example the 'Auto/biography' group of writers; Plummer 1995). This is now balancing the still-powerful sociological stress on the collective by reviving earlier social science interests in life stories and the creative role of individual actors (Plummer 1983). The trend has been further reinforced by the growing influence of oral history, giving access to ordinary people's subjective experience and their spoken life stories, and by the family history movement which has, among other things, encouraged older people to write the story of their lives. There is also the more general interest in documenting the experiences of hitherto 'invisible' and 'unsung' groups and individuals.

As a result the study of personal narratives is currently the focus of extensive interdisciplinary collaboration, involving, among others, anthropologists, psychologists, folklorists, historians, therapists and literary scholars as well as sociologists. And there are now many studies of personal narratives, not just from the past (like those quoted above) but of living people, young as well as old, in the present.

Our interest in personal narratives, however, is here not primarily in the direct 'factual' evidence that these stories can potentially give about the past or present (critically analysed and interpreted with due care, needless to say). This is one valid way to approach these narratives, of course. But more significant for present purposes is the role such narratives play in formulating and shaping their tellers' experience. Put another way, personal narratives can be regarded not as a simple reflection of life but rather as a way of constructing it.

This aspect is eloquently stated in Jerome Bruner's image of 'life as narrative'. Though coming from a background in psychology, Bruner draws on wide interdisciplinary insights and his influential writings have also been much read by sociologists. He puts forward what he calls a 'constructivist view of narrative', building on the philosophical position that 'world making' is a function of mind rather than a mere reflection of external reality. In a parallel way, he argues, autobiography 'should be viewed as a set of procedures for "life making"' (Bruner 1987: 11–12).

Bruner here gives a clear exposition of his view of 'life as narrative'. The telling of life stories represents not a mere expression of either outward reality or inner state but is itself an active form of structuring personal experience. He uses somewhat exaggerated language, perhaps, to convey his conclusion forcibly: 'A life as led is inseparable from a life as told ... A life is not "how it was" but how it is interpreted and reinterpreted, told and retold' (1987: 31).

Bruner states his position in blunt terms, but it is shared by other analysts of narrative (including several cited in his article). Indeed it is by now a familiar assumption in the comparative literature that narrative does not just reflect or report experience but also shapes it, as the Personal Narratives Group has it (1989). We formulate our experience through our knowledge of the stories of others and by telling our own stories, whether aloud or to ourselves. Indeed in one sense it is through that very storying that we experience – and recognize that experience – in the first place.

This 'meaning-ful' role of narrative is particularly visible when older people write or recount their life stories. The very fact of storying their life gives it validity, an enhanced sense of 'reality' and meaning. You may well have encountered this in your own everyday observation. It is also constructively utilized in therapeutic and gerontological contexts and in the 'reminiscence' movement (Bornat 1989). But the basic point is equally applicable to all ages. 'The self' is inevitably 'storied' and identity lies in the narratives constructed by the storying self. Structuring experience in narrative terms creates order out of chaos and gives meaning to what otherwise could only be experienced as anarchic or fragmented (as in Bruner 1987). The telling of personal stories above all, it seems, can formulate, justify and express personal experience through narrating the identity and self-understanding of the individual self.

With self-narratives, then, it could be argued that we have reached the irreducibly personal and individual. The representation is not being conveyed through the voices of outsiders, outshone by abstract academic stories (however authoritative-sounding), submerged into collective reports, or manipulated by external forces. Here we have the authentic structuring story in the very voice and words of the creative and thinking self-narrator.

There is much to be said for that formulation. Seeing the self as 'storied' does indeed give insight into subjective experience and personal interpretation in ways not provided for in other more generalizing and, as it were, 'outside' perspectives. It is then not just to such dimensions as the mass media, the political economy or even the conceptualizations of academics that we should look to see how culture is created or identities formed. We can also take account of self-narratives, a medium through which individuals at every level play a creative role in formulating both their own identities and, by extension, the culture in which they are participants.

So much would probably be widely agreed (if perhaps not always suffi-ciently emphasized). But taking the further step of suggesting 'irreducibility', 'authenticity' or total 'freedom' would be to overstate the case. For it does not follow that in personal narratives we have somehow finally reached the bedrock of something 'natural', unrelated to the culture in which the narrators carry out their lives. Indeed narrative scholars themselves – including Bruner – have been among the first to point to the culturally constructed conventions that emerge in personal narratives.

Self-narratives may at first sight seem too personal to contain recurrent stylistic or thematic patterns, or for us to apply the concept of 'genre' characteristics (for example, the genre of 'soap opera'). But life stories or personal narratives do seem to form a recognized genre in our culture. It is an 'informal' and often unwritten one, it is true. But the existence and – as it were – artistry of generic conventions is not confined to examples which have been visibly written down or formally published (a point nicely made in the title of Bakhtin's influential *Speech Genres*, 1986).

As with the narrators in Bruner's research, so too more widely: people quickly understand what is meant by telling a life story. Whether or not they have done so in that particular format before, they are ready and able to come up with intelligible versions of relevant narrative in culturally appropriate situations (you could test out this assessment from your own observation; for further discussion of the genres of 'life story' and other informal story-telling see Linde 1993, Abrahams 1985, Finnegan 1992). Genre is culturally defined – an art form rather than 'a fact of nature'. Thus we can identify the conventions which broadly make up the genre of soap opera. Similarly different genres of music each have their own conventions about their style, performance, audiences, etc. In the same way, approaching self-narrations from this viewpoint means that we can try to investigate the culturally defined conventions – their art, as it were – which narrators utilize to formulate their stories.

So though life stories and self-narrations are indeed personal, they also turn out to manifest a range of recurrent, culturally expected features. Some of these are widely found, perhaps even universal in human narrative. There are the structuring plot of the hero tale, the battle of good and evil, or the various protagonists and plot elements mentioned in Bruner's paper. Others are evident in particular historical periods or cultural situations. The short extract from Thomas Wood's life story quoted above is one example of this. It looks highly personal and transparent. But David Vincent's study of nineteenth-century working-class autobiographies, *Bread, Knowledge and Freedom* (1981) shows how, amid all the variety and personal idiosyncrasies of the stories, a series of stock themes come up time and again, principal among them being the struggle to self-improvement and success through self-education. One way of telling, experiencing and making sense of one's story in that particular social and historical context was to utilize this familiar plot.

Other recurrent themes pertain to specific groups, perhaps quite small ones. Luisa Passerini looked at the stories of imprisoned women members of leftist terrorist organizations like the Red Brigade in Italy in the 1970s and early 1980s, identifying 'the world of the imaginary' in their life stories. She is not by this implying they were 'false' or hallucinatory – as their opponents claimed – but rather describing how they related their own lives to recurrent images of:

> ... heroic stories of revolutionaries in other countries and other times; the legend of the hero or heroine who leaves home to help the oppressed ... the ideal of a small community united against the world, united beyond death; fables of the loyalty of mothers who do not abandon their defeated daughters, but are ready to give their lives for them. (Passerini 1990: 54)

The tellers had been imprisoned and defeated. Nevertheless their otherwise very diverse life stories showed how these women could define their reality by drawing on common mythic themes, 'a shared imaginary' (Passerini 1990: 54).

We can track other culturally constructed features in personal stories. There are, for example, the ways they are actually told or the influence of audience or setting on how they are formulated. The context in which nineteenth-century autobiographies were written and their authors' expectations about their audiences are also factors to be considered. But perhaps enough has been said to suggest that we cannot just take life stories as the 'natural' and unmediated effusions of asocial individuals. They remain uniquely personal, it is true – but they are also art-ful communications deploying recognized cultural conventions. And, as will emerge later, they also interact with other myths and tales of the culture.

The point here, then, is partly that other things are involved in personal narratives than just the individual teller. In other words, an 'intentional' analysis focusing only on the individual author is not sufficient. Equally important, personal stories are not just creations of a 'free' autonomous individual – one model of the self – but also of the cultural conventions he or she makes use of. The stories are themselves constructed cultural forms as well as constructing the life and experiences of their tellers.

The perspective here, then, involves viewing self-narratives neither as uncreative reflections of social attitudes nor as adjustments to external forces. Rather they are seen as culturally developed resources which – like language – people can draw on, manipulate and enact in the creation and experience of their storied lives.

Stories from home

The same narrative perspective can be extended to the contemporary lives around us, including those that have not hitherto been written down.

Among the many possible cases, let me again give some illustrations from the stories of people living in my own town of Milton Keynes. The tales are interesting in their own right. But at the same time as considering these personal narratives and their narrative analysis, you will also probably wish to bear in mind the broader issue of how far they can illuminate – or be illuminated by – the wider theories about the nature of the self.

For this we travel back to Milton Keynes, that famous (or notorious) 'new city' planned and started in the late 1960s as part of the British 'new town' policy of the time. We will be considering the stories of individuals in just one of the new housing estates built as part of the city's development.

Fishermead was one of the first 'grid squares' to be built in the new city, having been started in the mid-1970s. By the 1990s the estate had a poor reputation among other city-dwellers – a view that was not totally shared by its residents. One of these Fishermead residents was Shirley Lambert, whose story opened this chapter. But she was not the sole narrator, and widening the analysis to the personal tales of others who were also living in Fishermead at the time of their narrations (1994) can set her story in perspective.

Before turning to the stories themselves, perhaps I should briefly comment on the (justified) sociological question you are no doubt already asking: how were the stories recorded? As in Bruner's study, the speakers were invited to talk about their lives in short narrations only – a recording session of about an hour. The interviewer asked the occasional unpressing question about reactions to Fishermead or to Milton Keynes if this did not arise anyway, but in general the sessions were undirective.

The narrators were found largely by 'snowball' methods. That is, they were not selected as a statistically representative 'sample' – not in any case an appropriate method for the qualitative emphasis in most narrative analysis where the individuality of the speakers is likely to be as significant as any supposed 'typicality'. There was however some attempt to include a range of ages, backgrounds and educational experience. The narrators varied in fluency, with some more eager or available than others to talk about their experiences, perhaps explaining why women's narratives outnumbered men's. All the narrators included here were interested in telling their stories and were prepared to have them quoted (under pseudonyms, as here). Interestingly, most seemed not to find it strange to produce a relatively sustained account of their lives, even those for whom this was the first time they had presented it in this form (further background on the research and its methodology in Finnegan 1996, 1998).

A notable characteristic of the 35 self-narratives was their diversity. The stories depicted strikingly contrasting backgrounds, outlooks, experiences and speaking styles. The narrators had come to the area at different times, had different backgrounds, were more – or less – reflective, held contrary assessments of the locality, and had spent differing proportions of their lives in Milton Keynes. These highly individual stories and the lives with which the stories coincided make it difficult to reach definitive generalized conclusions about their 'identity', whether in 'essentialist' or 'subjective' terms.

The overwhelming impression, then, was of the richness of individual and differing personalities and of their formulation in narrative. Shirley Lambert's was perhaps a particularly memorable tale. But each story in its way presented its own personality and unique experience. It conveyed the voice of a thinking individual who, through personal memories and verbal articulation at one point in time, conveyed some sense of expressing meaning, of creating coherence, of somehow controlling and enunciating a distinctive place in the universe.

But beyond this personal diversity, some recurrent themes began to emerge. They were used in different ways in different tales, and no story contained all of them. But there did indeed seem to be a range of stock topics, motifs, protagonists and plot structures.

Let me illustrate a few of these recurrent narrative patterns, focusing especially on the devices used to produce tales which, despite their rapid and compressed telling, yet conveyed some sense of a coherent and intelligible story.

The motif of continuity from the past was one accepted rationale for the plot. Narrators often took it for granted that it would make sense both for themselves and their listeners if they linked important features of their lives with one or other of their parents or recounted their 'roots' and 'family tradition'. Stories commonly opened with an account of the teller's family origins and their inheritance from the past. The family and/or the place was presented as the ground from which the individual grew, in some sense explaining their life. Brenda Dawson's story started with her 'firmly working class roots' in Southall, portraying her family's background and her grandmother's tales:

> She was fascinating, and I used to listen stories of her childhood, and how she had to walk four miles to school and back in all weathers, and what they used to get up to. It was wonderful, it was like living history.

The thread running through another story was the teller's memory of his father who 'for me is still alive and guiding me'; 'I still thank him for all the things he did that made me the person that I am today'. Similar values came out in one narrator's 'Dorset pride', another's identity as a Londoner or a third's view of himself as 'proud to be a Somerset man'.

The continuities were sometimes presented as a kind of cyclical progression from the past and on to the future. Dennis Travers (a pseudonym again) told how his son had inherited his interest in art 'from me', while Alison Stanley explained:

We are a family of readers. ... All of us, my grandchildren are the same, and my children are the same, every house you go into in my family there are books.

On a lighter note, but personally important to the teller, Sally Vincent set her rotundity in longer perspective by her family inheritance: 'We are all little and round!'

This structuring from the past was usually presented as benign, but some stories narrated individuals' determination not to perpetuate some parental trait – an equally effective plot device. A major emphasis in Agnes Farley's story was on how her early life made her a 'rebel':

Well I was born in Devon in 1917 and I lived on a farm until I was twenty-three. ... And although I lived in an idyllic spot and really I didn't have anything to complain about, but on reflection I think I had a very lonely childhood because my brothers being that much older, and there were not a lot of children around, but also a very strong class distinction in that part of the world, and my mother was very aware of this and she insisted that I played only with the right children and this made life very difficult.

The prospects were in those days that one would live at home until one married, and most of my friends did just that. ... I think I was a bit cheesed in my teens and always wishing I was somewhere else, very much so. I was restricted, and I became so deceitful. I think if you live that existence you either become like a dummy or a rebel and I became a rebel.

Whether in positive or negative tone, narrators were taking for granted that an intelligible narrative structure, one shared with their listeners, was to set their experiences in the perspective of successive generations, framing their lives within a longer cycle of family continuity or discontinuity. The precise content of this continuity was unique to each teller. But the underlying framework was to convey the story not of a meaningless isolated individual from nowhere, but of someone with a just base for their own identity and place in history.

Another integrating device invoked some personal avocation or principle to give a continuing thread throughout the story. This could be a consuming interest held throughout life, like music, sport or religious adherence – recognized and value-laden pathways in our culture – depicted as a kind of signature tune with a meaning over and above specific events. Experiences around this continuing theme somehow conveyed a quasi-mythic flavour and were recounted with particular fluency and conviction.

An enthusiasm for music was one such theme. Seventy-two-year-old Andrew Cunningham was recovering from a stroke, finding it hard to speak, but became fluent once he started on music. His passion as a child was to learn drumming:

> I couldn't afford it, a pound an hour for lessons. Well, my dad said 'Well there you are, I can't pay for it, it's too much money'. I thought well blow it, I'll find my own way. So I taught myself by sound, and a record player, you used to put the HMV records on it. Seventy-eights. ... The thing I have never learned to do properly is a roll. Yeh, I couldn't do it now, cos of the hands you see, but I could do it slowly with a good drum kit. ... Course I had a drum kit and a great big bass drum like you see in The Salvation Army up there. ... And when the war came and I went to Wales and that was when I got in the band with the Hotshots. ... It was good it was.

His musical interests continued throughout his life.

Jonathan Tyler similarly spoke enthusiastically about music, this time in the role of listener. The pride of his life was his huge and well-used tape collection of some 120 composers. The same theme sets him in the longer scheme of family continuity:

> My love of music, well my mother used to play the piano very well, she was a good amateur pianist, and difficult things mostly Beethoven, and Schumann and that is probably what ignited it, and that probably put it in my brother's mind, because he played jazz all his life.

Music was an evocative metaphor for his own experience: 'I do like Milton Keynes now and I appreciate it, but it took time, it's like learning a new composer.'

Adherence to a particular religion and its discourse is another familiar framework for personal experience. One-hundred-year-old Timothy Hopkins was clear about its structuring significance in his life story. He started with his church upbringing, several times emphasizing his long membership of the local church choir in Dorset: 'I almost lived in the church, I loved it.' As a young man he lost an early job through loyalty to his own church's football team when he declined to play for the firm team. The same theme appeared in his vivid account of his godfather's voice saving him from death when his troop ship was torpedoed in the First World War. He couldn't swim much, and stood on deck wondering what to do:

> It may seem strange to you, but when I was born and I was going to die and my mother had sent for the minister to baptize me in my living room which he did, and she said we haven't got a godfather vicar and he said that's alright I'll be godfather and look after him all his life. That's the

point I'm getting at, I stood on this deck, not knowing, alone, a voice suddenly said to me 'Jump', and I turned around and there was nobody around, and it said 'Jump' and I ran to the side and I jumped over and down. The boat was going down the side and I jumped into this boat full of men and that saved my life, because we were only about twenty yards away, rowing, when the [ship] went down. ...

That voice I'm sure was my godfather, and it sounded like him to me afterwards, and they said it seems like you are imagining things, but I said no, I didn't, I distinctly heard this voice say 'Jump'.

Timothy was rescued and later spent time in a Cairo hospital, where the main episode he recounted was not his illness but his church involvement, for, as he put it, 'The church has been my life'. He struggled out to a church service, held in a marquee:

The minister spoke to me when the service was over, like they do at the door. He said 'Have you always attended church', and I said 'Yes I almost lived in the church'. He said, 'Well I wonder if you would help me with communion next Sunday, as my server?'. ... I did that and I wasn't very old and it was a great thing to me to serve communion in a marquee church.

Religious terminology continued throughout his story, and he finally reflected:

People say oh you are fond of flowers, and I say I am, I love flowers, to me they are one of God's gifts, from tiny little seeds you get wonderful flowers like that.

Music and religion are intelligible and familiar frameworks for a life story. Other preoccupations, however, are less widely recognized and so needed more elaboration to convey their centrality for the teller.

Peter Sutton's story, for example, was one of great upsets in some respects, but was bound together by one lifelong passion. He linked this to his family roots:

My mother was a great film fan, we never had a television until I was thirteen, she adored the cinema, and in London it was a – what is the word I am looking for? – a paradise. Film goers' delight. There were cinemas everywhere, so consequently I spent a lot of time going to the theatres, she loved live shows as well, my father was just not interested at all. That was where I started to get a great interest before I was even eight or nine, I was totally in love with the movies ... I have got to do these things called movies.

His plans to go to college were upset by his father's sudden death, and he had to take a factory job. But his love affair with film continued. Suddenly one Friday afternoon:

> I watched a chap of sixty-four, sixty-five coming up, he was planing a piece of wood [at the factory], a carpenter, and doing it at a fairly slow pace, and going backwards and forwards, and I was holding the broom, and I looked at him and I said to myself that man has been doing that for forty years. I am not going to do that for forty years, and I went into the office to Mr M – and I said I am so sorry but I don't think this is for me. ...
>
> I was out of work. I went to the Youth Unemployment and ... they said we don't know [how to get into the movies] the only way to do it is you will have to knock on a few doors, and go up to that place called Wardour Street, Soho, very nasty. And that is just what I did, got an underground train, a bus, underground train, down to Wardour Street, started at the bottom and ended up at the top at Oxford Circus, and half way down someone said they wanted a teaboy, a rewind boy, rewinding the films, and I said, 'Great terrific', £3.17s.6d. in those days, and I had a job. And that is how I started as a teenager.

His story continued about how he 'went on from there', his professional pride in film editing and the pressures of the job – 'beautiful, phenomenal'. Sad as he was over many disappointments, his devotion to film integrated – and justified – his narrated life.

The most prominent theme of all centred on the idea of the individual narrator and that narrator's sense of identity and control. In one sense this is almost too obvious to need stating. Speakers were invited to recount their personal experiences and – if only for grammatical reasons – the subject of many sentences was predictably 'I'. This indeed is the cultural convention we expect and exploit when we use the recognized autobiographical form of expression, one accepted framework through which individuality is experienced. But was there perhaps more to it than that? It was certainly striking how forcibly the concept of the individual emerged as a key structuring theme in these life stories.

This was conveyed in several ways. Some tales centred on the individual's character, one common mode for structuring a life story (Linde 1993: Ch. 5). This was sometimes related to the complementary theme of family background but also figured as a trait developed independently and individually.

Sally Vincent's story, for example, was notable for her confrontations, sticking up vociferously for her rights against neighbours, partners, relations, officials. Her narration was punctuated by explanatory asides: 'I am not a very patient person', 'I have never had patience, I ain't got none', 'You couldn't change me, not after all this time'. Similar – if less confrontational – was Brenda Dawson's assessment of herself as 'never very good at sort of lying quietly down like a doormat'. Though she stressed the frustrations of her life as an army wife, her story was partly structured round how she did indeed 'complain about things' and finally, by not being a 'doormat', won back an identity that she had 'kind of lost':

> It was very good because you know, I was sort of earning some money. It was just getting things sort of back for me – a life which wasn't just totally involved with children and looking after husband. ...
> It has been worthwhile.

Another prominent theme structuring the stories focused on the individual teller's positive action and enterprise – something more than just their enduring character. Shirley Lambert's story, already quoted, is one example. As she told it, despite her early (and partly continuing) misfortunes, she created her own life, exerted herself and step by step 'backed up courage' to help others and control events. Her initial foray into fostering 'made me feel proud that I could do something for somebody else what I couldn't do for my own family', and gradually her actions enabled her to avoid her violent father and help her younger sisters and mentally ill mother, as well as gaining the confidence to advise others about the courage needed when 'it's hard'. Her philosophy was 'to be my own boss, right, and try and earn money and help everybody around me, right'.

Rachel Jacobs' narrative was in its way similar. It presented some horrific personal experiences but also her enterprise in dealing with them. This concluded in a relatively happy ending as she met her successive problems by, in turn, founding her own firm, leaving the partner she felt had let her down (and being consequently left totally destitute), working as a cabbie to make ends meet, sacrificing that job to uphold the morals she wanted her children to observe, and exploring new ways of maintaining herself. Finally she had now found a group of congenial friends.

Not all examples were as explicitly articulated as these. Also it has to be said that the patterns detected in these otherwise very individual stories were emergent rather than elicited through direct questioning or systematic quantitative analysis. Nevertheless I was surprised by the prevalence of this theme. The stories regularly narrated active decisions and follow-through, from choosing to leave home for Milton Keynes at the age of sixteen or teenage persistence in finding a job to insisting on respect from others (the bakery shopkeeper who prided herself on forbidding swearing in her shop), supporting one's own children against others', or actively sticking up for a principle whatever the consequences.

This might not have been so. Given the social constraints we all labour under, not least these narrators (some of whom had confronted quite horrendous difficulties in their lives), the integrating narrative artistry might equally have deployed themes around a sense of powerlessness or the determining force of external events. There was something of this, but surprisingly little. The individual teller – in the role of hero – was presented as the essential reality of the story and took the central motivating role in its plot.

Stories involve other people and, particularly at certain life stages, the subject was sometimes 'we'. Nevertheless the active mover in these personal narratives was mostly 'I'. Stories recounted how this active 'I' detached itself to gain personal independence or achieve a particular aim. Leaving the parental home was one common turning point. Joy Osborne recounted her hesitations about leaving her foster home when she was eighteen but her satisfaction when she managed it:

> It took me three months for me to actually tell [my foster mother] that I had got this flat … because she had been so good to me, and I felt like I was letting her down by leaving in a way. In the end I told her and she was over the moon for me and she came over and saw it and so I moved in. But although I moved in, I spent most of the time out sleeping at other people's houses because Christ, I was frightened really.
>
> Eventually I remember being round a friend's house and I said I think I'll go home tonight, I am not going to stay, I'm going to go home, and that was the beginning of me getting into the homely type thing, and wanting to decorate and getting me stuff together. I was eighteen then, I got it just after I was eighteen, and I really enjoyed it, it was like you know this is my own pad.

Individual action and control were expressed even in tales recounting external constraints or disappointments, things 'happening' rather than consciously planned. Brenda Dawson's tale of forced and reluctant moves as an army wife also told how she dealt with them, while Joyce Lacey immediately amplified her 'not so much a decision as something that happened' by '– and making the most of what happened'. Shirley Lambert's tale ended with the reflective commentary on her scarcely easy life:

> Everybody is allowed a chance, and I didn't have the chance and I gave myself the chance though and I think if I can do it anybody can.

Lesley Lambert was one of very few who directly referred to her lack of power:

> I feel like I should try and do something [for Milton Keynes], but what can you do, when you have an idea and you go somewhere with it, they beat you down, because they are like oh you are just small fry, once you try you just get kicked down, and you can't win, unless you have got money.

But she then followed this by a long episode depicting her effectiveness in another context – 'trivial' to some readers, perhaps, but notably one of the liveliest and most fluent episodes in the narration:

> A friend of mine that I worked with told me that there was a house going and so we moved in, it was a really big house, three bedrooms and it was a three storey house, the wallpaper was dire and it was really really bad it was half pink and half blue, and I used to think who in their right mind would paint their wallpaper half pink and half blue, it was like a nightmare, and so we got to painting it straight away, and there is so many good memories in that house. ...
>
> We had this brainwave that we were going to decorate the little toilet, and we wanted to do something really different and Paula is really arty and I said why don't we print handprints going up the wall, we can have a little border and then they could go up the wall, and she said that is a good idea we could do it in the middle of the wall and go up and then she said no, I think we should paint our hand and stick handprints on the wall, so we got this paint and painted our hands and stuck our hands up the wall, and we got our friend's little brother and we painted his feet and stuck his footprints up the wall, and we signed it and it was really like, we were proud of our toilet, and everybody that came round we would say come and see our toilet ... and they said wow. We were really proud of that toilet. ... The things we used to do, the memories are really good in that house, excellent. ... We were proud of our little house, it was nice.

The story ended with the narrator's confident plans for the future: 'it has all worked out really well'.

An account of struggles or problems can be used to convey a sharp sense of individual control, as with 11-year-old Andrew Cunningham's determination to learn to drum. Other stories elaborated their narrator's 'struggle', 'hard work', or 'hard times'. Individual determination was emphasized in the vivid accounts of divisive quarrels, often between partners, with their 'I said'/'(s)he said' interchanges, or of parents sticking up for their own children against others: they may not be angels, but 'I am a mum and will protect them to the end ...'. Jill Blackwell, when asked 'Has it made a difference to your life, being in Milton Keynes?', responded in words recalling a motif evident in many stories: 'Yeh it has made a difference, well, I have made the difference, I have gone out and made the difference.'

This sense of personal control was partly conveyed through the personal motivation and interventions depicted in the stories' events. Partly too, it came from the control that, as evidenced in other research on narrative, lies in the personally activated processes of memory and narration, themselves playing a part in shaping the world, and from the coherence that perhaps emerges through the very process of creative retrospection.

It was the self-reflective way stories were told and their small throwaway comments as much as the actions themselves that conveyed this personal determination and energy. 'It's a tough world', commented one narrator, while Shirley Lambert reflected that 'If people don't help themselves ... they will go under'. Bessie Wyatt summed up her story about getting her foot on the ladder, progressing upwards, loving her job and divorcing her husband in difficult circumstances by 'If you want something you've got to work for it'.

This individual action and control was sometimes formulated through plots that are also well known from other types of stories. One form was that of a hero's progress upwards, re-enacted in the narrator's life. The 'final' ending might not yet be revealed but the successes of the present moment represented a kind of closure. Lucy Dale struggled for – and achieved – her educational qualifications, Agnes Farley her independence, Brenda Dawson her 'identity'. Several narrators told of beginning from almost nothing in material, educational or personal terms and gradually winning through. Elsie Simmons recalled moving into her present house:

> There was a cardboard box. I'll never forget it. All my dishes in a cardboard box! We set the telly on it. We had the cheek to go and buy a tablecloth to sit on top of it. Oh God. Oh, I used to be really embarrassed to open the door to somebody and say 'Oh, come in'. It was alright if you went upstairs for there was a carpet though we were all sleeping on the floor. It took me years to get where I am.

Fishermead was regularly classed as a sink estate by outsiders, for the dregs. But the tellers living there could – and did – also experience their lives as exemplifying the narrative themes of progress and personal control. They were creatively drawing on the narrative resources developed in our culture as they told and experienced the story of their lives.

The move through life was also sometimes presented as a kind of adventure tale. Some recounted pioneering days in the early development of estates in Milton Keynes, of coping with mud, new friends, and the absence of shops or hospital. Others related childhood adventures, the 'enjoyment' and challenges of parenthood, job, or a particular house or area. Accounts of excitement and enjoyment marked out particular stages of life – and thus of the plot – and again foregrounded the concept of the self-conscious reflecting individual.

Life imaged as a journey of self-discovery came into several stories, the narrator reflecting back on the stages of a personal voyage. The story progresses through episodes of making mistakes and learning from them, of gathering strength – 'becoming stronger and more resolved than carrying on the wishy washy existence I was beforehand' – or of changing views at different stages: 'What was so important isn't quite so important when you get older and you have different values actually' (Agnes Farley). One narrative was shot through with 'learning about myself as a person', and concluded that her recent visit to America 'really helped me to grow as a person', quoting a friend's comment that she was:

> ... almost like this little flickering light and you have just come brighter. ... I am really chuffed with myself, and I have been back eight months now, and I have done everything I said I was going to do.

Rachel Jacobs reflected on her own story, one with many trials:

> It is now really that I feel good about Milton Keynes, I feel like I am home. ... It has actually been a personal journey, not just a financial one. ... And I suspect that in five years' time I suppose I will see where I am now as just another stage along the way.

Unlike many written or fictional stories, these personal stories were not closed – in one sense the end had yet to come, for the living teller continued. Tales thus stopped rather than ended. But some tellers did introduce explicit closing comments or conclusion-like reflections. This was particularly noticeable in older people's narratives which often convey a greater sense of a 'completed' story than those by young and middle-aged narrators. This broadly applies to the Milton Keynes narratives. Emma Hardy concluded: 'It's not a very exciting life, but when we look back on it we have such great memories, it's so lovely ... It wasn't a wasted life', while Frank Dyer reflected: 'I have lived through a period of life [with many changes] ... I think I have lived through sixty years of the greatest advancement in all respects, and I treasure it.' Centenarian Timothy Hopkins was well justified in concluding: 'Well that's my story ... and as I say I went through life, and that is exactly my life story.' But some younger people's stories too conveyed something of the same quality, as in the conclusion to Shirley Lambert's tale above. Several narratives conveyed a quiet end as the narrators expressed themselves as content with their present state; others rounded it off by looking to the future.

These narrations did indeed seem to fulfil for their tellers something of the role identified in the comparative literature of shaping, not just reflecting, experience. Both at the time of the recording and from follow-up discussion later, it was evident that they found having told their stories satisfying, sometimes surprising. It provided a kind of proof of the reality and significance of their lives and their capacity to, in a sense, control and make them meaningful through the creative process of verbalized self-reflection.

The various conventions for telling life stories also carry some measure of implicit generalization: this is what makes them intelligible to both tellers and listeners. The personal tales, of course, tell of unique individuals and their experiences, but the overtones of their recurrent themes draw the tale beyond the immediate situation. The shared familiarity of their recognized plots and figures takes them beyond just the deeds of single individuals – even as at the same time they communicate precisely because they present the accepted general motif of individuals' deeds. It is striking how between them these personal stories – in contrast to many traditional academic accounts – so clearly project a theoretical model emphasizing the significance of the individual, of the self-conscious, creative self.

Stories, tellings, and more stories

Before leaving these personal narratives, I want briefly to draw attention to two other of their features: their ambiguous nature as 'texts' and/or 'performances' and their relation to other forms of stories in and about Milton Keynes.

First, then a further point about the construction of personal stories. The published literature sometimes implies that people are constantly telling their life stories or waiting to do so, a worked-out and somehow independent monologue somewhere lurking in their minds. But the self-narratives considered here – and, I suggest, others too – did not function like that. Their genesis seemed to lie less in bounded, sustained and fully verbalized texts than in continuing smaller dialogues, variable tellings, bitty interchanges, responses to questions: a potential which could then be verbalized – more or less coherently and lengthily – in response to a particular situation,

The concept of talking about their own life and memories was not an unfamiliar notion to the tellers recorded here. But few, if any, had actively narrated their lives in the concentrated forum of a one-hour session (though Timothy Hopkins had previously written the story of his life). When it came to the occasion of recording – essentially a dialogue situation, remember, interacting with another interlocutor rather than a single-line monologue text – some tellers formulated a relatively sustained and fluent story with little prompting. They had doubtless told parts of it before in other situations. Some had perhaps formed the habit – or the need – of articulate justification of their lives, or reached a stage of life (old age and grandparenthood in particular) when reflecting back on their lives is an expected activity. Others were less fluent overall, though sometimes very articulate on particular episodes. Some tellers invoked more interaction with the interviewer than those who had in one sense 'rehearsed' aspects of their tales before. Many were surprised and pleased by their capacity to tell their story, commenting that they had never done it in that way before. But all had resources which they could deploy to do so. All responded to the occasion of the interview by formulating the story in a form which – fluent or not – both told of their lives and was unique to that specific occasion.

The stories here were thus each delivered on one particular occasion, and with the performance attributes typical of an interactive process rather than a fixed text. They were not carefully meditated or sustained narratives, nor were they deliberately worked up and 'improved' between a series of recording sessions (as were some of the stories analysed in the literature). They drew, indeed, on a combination of personal experience and accepted conventions for such tellings, but had probably not been told in that particular form before, nor perhaps would be again.

Such oral narrations thus need to be pictured less on the model of a fixed written text than as a kind of store of accepted resources for personal story-telling. Speakers drew variously on these resources in interaction with their own experiences and perspectives to formulate a story – long or short – with varying emphases and selection depending on the audience and the occasion. The recurrent themes, plots and protagonists of the stories are no less significant, however, for being essentially activated in performance rather than in closed textual form. Indeed the oral delivery context lays all the more onus on the individual teller's creativity in drawing on both conventional store and personal originality on the live occasion of performance.

There is also a second issue. So far the focus has been on the personal stories themselves. However there were also, of course, other concurrent stories with which these self-narratives interacted – and interacted within the context of the specificities of time and place.

The stories told in our culture are multiple, and – as emerged earlier – are of many different kinds and told at many levels. We can think not only of the unending series of differing personal tales, but also of the overarching myths shaping and expressing both widespread human assumptions (perhaps) and the contingent viewpoints of specific cultures about, say, the nature of human society or of personhood. Added to these are the interpretations of contrasting groups and sections, both general and in relation to specific events or situations, and – not to be forgotten among the manifold stories which influence our views – the many storied interpretations of academics in all their diversity.

Relevant too for these personal narratives were other stories specific to Milton Keynes. These stories took a variety of forms. One powerful – but not universally accepted – story was the upbeat success tale told by and about the planners of the new city, led by the heroic Milton Keynes Development Corporation to its happy conclusion. Then there was the alternative version of the new city as a routinized, cultureless, over-bureaucratized wasteland, bereft equally of human artistry or community roots, a tale often symbolically summarized through the image of the artificial 'concrete cows' located in one of the city's parks. This story above all was the popular one in the mass media. It also fitted well with the pessimistic stories of much urban sociology and the deeply engrained English myth of the battle between rural 'natural' community and intrusive 'artificial' town. Or again – and less widely known outside Milton Keynes – there was the emergent narrative currently being constructed by local historians and artists eager to create a storied history for Milton Keynes, a story which could celebrate not only its part in the longer-scale historical diversities of Buckinghamshire over the centuries, but also the personal deeds and adventures of its inhabitants. All these many tales contributed to the store of cultural resources on which personal narrators could draw in formulating their personal self-narrations.

Exactly what part was played by these many available tales or their tellings (and by which) remains, of course, one key issue for debate. That question could scarcely be settled just by considering the tales of thirty-five inhabitants of one English town in 1994. But neither, I would remark, could it be settled alone by abstract stories that paid no attention to such real-life stories of ordinary people. So let me add that one surprising feature about the personal narratives I studied was how unpredictably and variously – indeed how little – they drew directly on the more general Milton Keynes stories. Certainly there were the recurrent themes discussed above, and some others too. But in the end the most striking feature about these personal stories remained their individual diversity rather than their sameness.

The overall impression was of individual narrators moulding their own stories – deploying accepted narrative conventions, it is true, but putting their own individual stamp on their stories rather than merely reproducing other (arguably more 'powerful') stories in the culture. And insofar as they did draw on more widespread cultural stories – the varying different theories about the nature of the self, for example – they did so differentially and selectively among a plurality of differing tales. The two-sided models implied, for example, in the ruler/worker dichotomies of traditional Marxism or even sometimes in more open notions like 'reflection' or 'resistance', do not fit the multiple complexity of the resources on which these tellers drew.

So these stories were both personal but yet not purely personal. In that they were cultural constructs, not 'natural' phenomena, their tellers were able to draw from a store of themes and generic conventions which gave them a culturally recognized art form to interpret and articulate personal experience and the development of a life – a store which in principle included all the multiple stories in diverse voices to be encountered in Milton Keynes and beyond. But this did not stop them from also being individual. These storied formulations were essentially generated and realized by their tellers rather than being the results of control by others or the products of outside forces. Influenced and shaped they certainly were by the emergent store of generic conventions and narratives in the culture which these personal stories in turn helped to generate. But they also represented an intensely personal creation, not just an automatic reflection, of the cultural resources which both moulded and were moulded by the personal tellings.

4

Forget the words ...:
It's *performance!*

This chapter takes up the point about language-as-performed from the earlier discussion and relates it to broadly pragmatist views of language in a discussion of the arts and actions of linguistic performing. It goes on to explain, with examples drawn from both fieldwork and reading, the significance of a performance approach to human expression and experience.

The tale of a snuff-taker

Hey! Attention you. Everyone come and listen ...
I am Dauda, the son of Fanneh Konteh of Kamabai. I've come.
Well now, a story for you oh! Listen, won't you! Listen!
A human once came out on earth ...

The voice of Dauda Konteh the blind teller rang out in a West African village, prelude to his story, while the audience gathered slowly to listen and join in the performance.

How should we understand such performances? The standard method is to transcribe, translate and print them, approaching them essentially as written texts. Here I refer to three contrasting examples to suggest a different angle, complementing script-based perspectives by the more anthropological approach that foregrounds performance and context. In this, meaning is seen as actualized not just in entextualized words but *also* as lying in a range of communicative channels, participants, settings, ideologies, diverse generic conventions, and events themselves.

Dauda's narration was one of many tales being told by Limba-speaking narrators in northern Sierra Leone in the 1960s that I recorded during anthropological fieldwork in the 1960s.[1] Dauda was known for his clever

---

1 Recounted and discussed in Finnegan 1967, 2007.

plots and effectiveness in exploiting Limba performance arts; like most of his audience, he did not read or write. One of his hallmarks was to intersperse his narrations with asides like 'and I was there too, peeping at them' – striking indeed, since everyone present knew he was blind. This time it was to be an uproarious tale about a ludicrous fellow addicted to snuff and the audience was already agog for what they knew would be an entrancing and engaging occasion.

The art of a snuff taker

Dauda gets into his narrative in typical Limba style, his voice rising in pitch, volume and rapidity to convey his hero's absurdly extreme personality.

> Well then, a human once came out on earth. He was called Daba. Daba. Daba. He was a great great great taker of snuff, the greatest taker of snuff on the earth ...

He depicts Daba going round the local chiefs asking for snuff, causing great merriment as he irreverently conveys the chiefs' characters through voice and mien. In a series of parallel episodes, characteristic of this Limba genre, Dauda enacts dialogues between Daba and each chief in turn: Daba pretend-begs but scornfully rejects the housefuls(!) of snuff he's offered. The action is vividly conveyed through Dauda's speed, repetitions, abrupt shouts or stops, intonation, exaggeration, gestures and facial expression, his voice and body dramatizing the action while also slily mimicking (satirizing?) the Limba formalities of greeting and begging. The audience is part of it all, co-creators of the performance, with exclamations, anticipation, laughter, repetition. At the crucial point in each episode they join in a repeated song, ending up with *maröö*, the laughter-provoking sound of Daba's nostril sniffing up the snuff:

> *Daba yo, Daba yo, Daba yo*
> *Taking snuff*
> *Daba yo, Daba yo*
> *na maröö!*

Part of the occasion is their active enjoyment, near-dancing, in their singing, repeated and repeated between teller and chorus until Dauda breaks in loudly with the next episode. At last Daba overreaches himself – 'I stood behind and heard him' adds Dauda – sniffs, and to the hilarity of all falls down dead.

In printed format the plot looks simple, even stupid. A literal transcription might well seem to lend evidence, for those with such expectations, of the 'crudeness' of African tales. And yet, as noted in Chapter 1, this was one of the most subtle and hilarious narrations I encountered during my time with the Limba. Why?

The answer, of course, lay in its performance; its meaning and art emerge through its delivery, occasion and multiple participants. It was actualized in Dauda's creative marshalling of sound, sight and movement to exploit the genre's conventions, the sonic nuances, reduplications, mimicry, characterization, gesture, direct speech, working of the audience, songs, atmosphere, and the bodily involvements of the participants, both teller and co-performing audience. What looks trite on the printed page can be profound, allusive, and full of both sharply observed individuality and universal drama on the actual occasion.

And then, of course, the 'words' I've given weren't actually what I heard – that was in Limba. So the 'quotations' here are merely my translations, shaped as always by the translator's own preconceptions and already inevitably altering the original beauties and subtleties. Furthermore, enclosing this multidimensional and multi-participant performance within the narrow one-voiced medium of writing was yet a second kind of translation – a new creation in its own right perhaps, but definitely not the full substance of the multimodal performance I heard and saw on that day in January 1964 in the village of Kamabai. As with other attempts to capture the magic of live story-telling, in the cage of linear print my transformations suppress so much of the art – one reason why collections of African narratives often convey such a thin, even demeaning, impression of these rich oral genres.

I picked this particular tale because the creativity of performance comes through more clearly where there is relatively little linguistic text to distract us into thinking that that is the primary essence. Some stories were, in fact, much more verbally elaborated, delivery skills up to a point varied, and each occasion had its own mix of features and of more, or less, engaged participants. But multimodal performance was consistently an expected, and actualized, characteristic of this Limba genre. The univocal linear text – the focus of many approaches to literature and the element captured on the written page – can give us, at best, only one of its dimensions.

Poems of a dub artist

The second example is very different in its social and historical setting, participants, and generic conventions – dub poetry by the contemporary Jamaican-Canadian poet Lillian Allen. First, from her 'Birth Poem':

An mi labour an mi labour an mi labour
An mi labour an mi labour an mi labour:
An mi bawl Whai
An mi push an mi push an mi push

An mi push an mi push an mi push
AN MI PUSH
An baps she born
An it nice yu see
an she sweet yu see
This little girl mi call Anta.
(extract, Habekost 1993: 206).

The text doesn't amount to much: just a woman recalling being in labour, yelling *'whai'*, pushing, then *baps*! her daughter is born, isn't she sweet. But so much is created in performance. It starts with a rhythmic musical beat, setting the scene then running through the whole, and a gentle chorus about 'this little girl mi call Anta'. Then comes the poet's voice – her actual one – portraying the length and suffering and intensity of the labour, words mingling with – formed through – groans, sighs, shouts, repetitions, crescendos ... As one admirer describes:

> Allen's breathtaking performance of 'Birth Poem' never fails to mesmerize her audiences. It is obvious what this piece means to its author. Pushing herself and her baby poetically towards birth, Allen shows what an accomplished performer she is: her face distorts in pain, her gestures provide staccato punctuation as she rants a fast, rolling wave-like rhythm culminating in the onomatopoeic 'baps'. [Then] ... the poet relaxes into smiles, and, in a happy melodious Jamaican voice, celebrates her baby. (Habekost 1993: 206)

Then back to the chorus, 'this little girl mi call Anta'. It is emphatically not just words-as-written but the intense, forceful, vehement, repeated and repeated and repeated 'an mi labour and mi labour and mi labour' as the meaning grows beyond the birth of one small baby into the labour and strength of the women whose cause Allen's poetry promotes and celebrates.

'Dub' poetry[2] is rooted in the popular musical culture of Jamaica. Presented in Creole, the local english vernacular, it developed into a performance genre from the 1970s, initially linked to disc jockeys' practice of 'dubbing' words in over recorded reggae rhythms: riddim, the Creole spelling, has strong associations with black identity, struggle, and resistance to the dominant culture. Performance, live or recorded, is paramount but dub poets sometimes also publish their poetry. It also came to be broadcast and performed in more commercial multicultural settings through audio, video and film to changing (and sometimes disapproving) audiences, disseminated not just in Jamaica but overseas, including the UK.

2   Described in such works as Brown 1987, Cooper and Devonish 1995, Glaser and Pausch 1994, Habekost 1993, Morris 1999.

Lillian Allen, Jamaican-born but now settled in Canada and well known for her distinctive black feminist voice, exploits the fertile resources of this dub tradition in her own style. Her quasi-intoning delivery with its caressed Creole pronunciations is intertwined with non-verbal voiced sounds, with interjections, cadences, mimicry and vocal startlements. She exploits gesture, facial expression and body language, deploying seen and heard movement and mood, with a pervading musical frame as drum and bass rhythms reverberate through the bodies of the participants.

> *drum beat drum beat*
> *pulse beat*
> *heart beat*
> *riddim an' hardtimes riddim an' hardtimes*
> *riddim an' hard*
> *hard*
> *hard*
> (Allen 1993: 64 [*Riddim an' hardtimes,* final stanza])

The poetic impact comes though the beat, her embodied presence, and her creative use of pacing, silence and sound, not least her memorable swoop up in the 'times' of 'hardtimes' and the echoic dying-away of 'hard, hard, hard, hard ...'.

'Nellie Belly Swelly' is more verbally extended:

> *Nellie was thirteen*
> *don't care 'bout no fellow*
> *growing in the garden*
> *among the wild flowers*
> *she Mumma she dig & she plant*
> *nurtures her sod*
> *tends her rose bush*
> *in the garden pod*
> *lust leap the garden fence*
> *pluck the rose bud*
> *bruk it ina the stem*
> *oh no please no*
> *was no self defence*
> *oh no please no*
> *without pretence*
> *offered no defence*
> *to a little little girl*
> *called Nellie*
> *Nellie couldn't understand*
> *Mr. Thompson's hood*

so harsh, so wrong in such an offensive
Nellie plead, Nellie beg
Nellie plead, Nellie beg
but Mr. Thompson's hood
went right through her legs
knowing eyes blamed her
Nellie disappeared from sight
news spread wide
as the months went by
psst psst psst Nellie belly swelly
Nellie belly swelly Nellie belly swelly
children skipped to Nellie's shame
Nellie returned from the night
gave up her dolls
and the rose bush died
Nellie Momma cried Nellie Momma cried
little Nellie no more child again
No sentence was passed
on this menancing ass
who plundered Nellie's childhood
In her little tiny heart
Nellie understood war
She mustered an army within her
strengthened her defence
and mined the garden fence
No band made a roll
skies didn't part
for this new dawn
in fact, nothing heralded it
when this feminist was born.
(Allen 1993: 25–7)

This could certainly be approached as a poetic text primarily existent in its printed words. But it was composed for and in performance. Its meaning is also created in its music, audience reactions, Nellie's begging, the (non-printed) repetitions, the unverbalized gossiping scorn over Nellie's condition, the beautiful Creole pronunciations with evocations far beyond the words-as-written, and the repeated and repeated chanting of the children's gleefully mocking 'Nellie belly swelly, Nellie belly swelly ...'. The poem exists in all these, not just in writing. Allen has also published recordings and printed versions of her poems. Unlike the African tales, this is not transformation by outsiders; but it is not unproblematic either. As she prefaces her collection *Women Do This Every Day* (1993):

Because words don't (always) need pages, I have published extensively in the form of readings, performances and recordings. I have been reluctant to commit my poetry to the page over the years because, for the most part, these poems are not meant to lay still.

As I prepared poems for this collection, I was required to 'finalize' pieces I had never imagined as final. Like a jazz musician with the word as her instrument, reading and performing these poems is an extension of the creative and creation process for the work. In some ways, I had to reverse this process to 'finalize' these poems for print; finding their written essence; pages do need words. (Allen 1993: Preface)

Such publications need to be set in the Jamaican context. 'Standard' English had long been the 'proper' form, with Creole denigrated or ignored. In the struggle over language, publishing poetry in Creole was a political, not just a literary act.

Not that Caribbean writers have used Creole-indicative spellings in either consistent or phonetically exact ways, nor do such spellings always appear throughout a poem even when its performance is unmistakably Creole. What they do however is provide aural hints of Creole speech and, equally important, symbolize and assert the rights of the 'non-standard' – an eye token, visually displayed, of the oral powers and traditions of Jamaican speech, 'making concrete a resistance to exclusion' (Casas 1998: 7). Allen's evocation of Creole speech in 'Riddim an' hardtimes' is 'a defiant gesture ... [invoking] the sound of Caribbean creole in the diaspora in the 1990s' (Casas 1998: 19). Like other dub poets Allen also uses spellings, creative typographical formats and crafted layout to visually signal and play on the emotive relations between orality and 'scriptism', Creole speech and 'standard' writing, 'high' and 'low', 'vulgar' and 'respectable'.

In one sense, her text now exists in its own right, with all its visual play and multimodal resonances, insisting on its right to appear in printed format, Creole-oral intermixtures and all. So yes, it is the words too, and for Allen these are one important element – her performances are of poems after all, not of newspaper columns. But they are complemented by the performanced arts of both live delivery and broadcast or recorded presentations. And anyone with experience of her stunning performances would surely find it impossible to approach the printed text of, say, 'Riddim an' hardtimes' without echoic resonances interwoven with the aural and visual overtones of spellings and printed format: the performance in the text.

And carols

Finally, a short mention of the carols sung in the chill of English Decembers – for contrary to what is sometimes assumed, it is not just in

Africa-linked forms that performance is significant. Usually a sequence of verses to a repeated tune, carols are sung in a plethora of contexts over the Christmas season: in broadcasts and recordings as well as live performances; in great cathedrals, local church services, schools, homes and streets; by jointly singing groups or congregations (a very common context) or by sophisticated four-part choirs with near-professional soloists; sometimes as unaccompanied voices but often interwoven with organ, piano, guitar or other instruments. They are a prominent part of the English Christmas.

In these largely literate settings people mostly rely on written texts, and the words – sometimes anonymous, more often by named authors – are as a matter of course encapsulated in print. Their themes cluster around the baby Jesus: born in a stable, laid in a manger, tended by his mother Mary, and acclaimed by angels and eastern kings. There are new carols too, but particularly often performed are long-established favourites like 'O come, all ye faithful' with its gender-divided chorus 'O come let us adore him', sung at just about every church service over Christmas; the jointly sung but also sometimes soloist-delivered 'Once in royal David's city / Stood a lowly cattle shed'; the cheerful 'Hark! the herald angels sing / Glory to the new-born king'; and 'The first Nowell the angels did say' with its (often) descant-decorated chorus. 'I wish you a merry Christmas ...' is sometimes formally sung in complex musical settings but also good for child carollers collecting around neighbourhood doors, and 'Away in a manger' is famously the first carol small children learn and perform. In all these, the words are indeed an important and explicitly recognized element. But this genre is also – and typically – realized through its music, singing, widespread participation and atmosphere of festival.

In a way, every enactment of these or other carols is unique. Each performance has its own features, both expected and specific to the occasion: its mix of communicative channels; its particular place and timing; its participants, with their own perspectives and struggles among themselves (some perhaps happy to admire, others impatient with a conductor foregrounding choir rather than congregation; some more enamoured than others of festive associations with celebration, family, 'good cheer'...); the detailed performance arrangements, music, singing, colour – all the elements that enter into one given event.

Yet each occasion can be multilayered too, as enactments from past and present meet. 'Performance, even in its dazzling physical immediacy, drifts between present and past, presence and absence, consciousness and memory', Elin Diamond writes, and 'embeds features of previous performances' (1996: 1). For those acquainted with English carols, it would be hard to participate in any rendering of the well-known examples, even to read their words, without creatively entexturing the experience with a host of multimodal resonances.

Carols are just one example of sung art, for lyrics – poems-set-to-music – are a common format for the art of English, even if often brushed aside or conceptualized as essentially their written words. Here too, as in our earlier examples, verbal language is indeed one dimension – but not necessarily the only or even the most salient one. From Elizabethan madrigals, Shakespeare's lyrics or George Herbert's hymns to calypsos, Bruce Springsteen's lyrics or the latest pop idol's songs, their reality lies not just in entextualized words but also (varying with genre and context) in a range of multimodal dimensions such as musical enactment, instrumentation, participants, chorus–leader interactions, visual components, and/or expression through dance, rhythm and bodily dynamic. These can be integral rather than peripheral to their ontology.

To conclude

Comparable approaches can be taken to other genres as well, performed or performable, read or heard, past or present, English or non-English – including, no doubt, many with which the reader may be more directly familiar than the examples here.

Here as elsewhere, performance and text are not after all two independent entities, but complementary dimensions of verbal art: in one way entextualized as words, written or writable, in another realized through multidimensional enactment, or, more elusively, through the 'en-performancing' of text, the 'now' when the reader personally experiences and (re-)creates it, intershot as this is with evocations beyond the immediate moment. Direct and imagined memories of experienced performances drench the text for us, whether from Shakespeare play, read-aloud novel, dub poem or Beatles lyric. Even an unfamiliar text can call up personal or shared resonances from a multiplicity of situations and experiences, while for poetry we regularly create its sonic presence, not just attend to its visual layout – again, the performance in the text. We may screen all these out of our consciousness, but they are there in our lived experience.

'Performance' is not some simple 'add-on' to text, but a range of multimodal dimensions through which verbal art exists. Not all will be present, or equally present, on any one occasion or in every genre. But whatever the example, our grasp of its ontology and meaning can be enriched by exploring the kinds of dimensions sketched here: the immediate and imagined settings; participants; diverse multimodal actualities and resonances (not just acoustic and visual, but sometimes tactile and somatic too); the situations and ideologies (perhaps contested or multiply interpreted); and the generic conventions creatively marshalled in both unique and recurrent ways.

Does all this sound too multidimensional to grasp? But in practice, whether we consciously notice it or not, it is something people are in one way or another engaged in every day, practising and experiencing the literary arts of England and of the world.

5

Reclothing the 'oral'

Is oral language different from written? Do we need to add special factors to analyse oral literature? And what difference, if any, does literacy make?

It is Jack Goody who, in Walter Ong's train, has most forced anthropologists and their followers to face up to these questions. Enormously influential but never uncontroversial, Goody's insights and claims have released a flood of publications from the 1960s to the present, supporting, challenging and interacting with his developing positions.

Most of the discussion has revolved round issues about literacy. This chapter focuses on the other end, the concept of 'oral'.

Uncovering the oral

For this, Goody's works have been seminal. Many others before him had, of course, concerned themselves with verbal art, oral tradition or vocal communication, and there was already extensive scholarly research within (for example) philology, folklore, classical studies and linguistics. But a new impetus was set by his essay with Ian Watt on the consequences of literacy (1963) and his edited *Literacy in Traditional Societies* (1968).[1]

The particular challenge was to anthropologists, with their focus on 'traditional' 'pre-literate' societies where writing was either (apparently) absent or, if present, to be brushed aside as artificial intrusion. I well remember the startling impact of that 1968 volume. At first it seemed near-revolutionary that the study of *writing* itself could and should be part of the anthropological enterprise. But in Goody's much-quoted statement:

---

1 Goody's interest arose, he once told me, from a period in a prisoner-of-war camp in Italy during the Second World War when, deprived of reading material, he started to ponder the merits and demerits of literacy, an interest that remained with him throughout his life.

At least during the past 2,000 years, the vast majority of the peoples of the world (most of Eurasia and much of Africa) have lived ... in cultures which were influenced in some degree by the circulation of the written word, by the presence of groups or individuals who could read and write ... Even if one's attention is centred only upon village life, there are large areas of the world where the fact of writing and the existence of the book have to be taken into account, even in discussing 'traditional' societies. (1968: 4–5)

This was more than just an injunction to include writing within ethnographic research, important as that was. It also directed attention to writing as a topic in its own right, worthy of comparative investigation across 'traditional' and 'modern' societies alike, and initiated Goody's long quest for the differences between oral and literate cultures, soon to be taken up by scholars from a wide range of disciplines. And if 'writing' was a fit object for social scientific study, then the same was true of the unwritten, the 'oral' – a then-revolutionary project. Orality, too, could not just be taken for granted – just 'there' as the bedrock, unnoticed because assumed to be universal in traditional society; it demanded study as the counterpart to literacy in the study of human modes of communication. Orality, too, was – in a favourite Goody phrase – a 'technology of the intellect'.

Goody's work interacted with parallel streams gathering momentum from the 1960s onwards. Parry, Lord and their followers were uncovering 'oral-formulaic' features in Yugoslav heroic poetry ('oral literature') and thence on into classical, Old English and biblical studies, and more. McLuhan and Ong stirred the imagination about the qualities of oral as against written expression. De-colonization gave newly independent nations an additional interest in recording and dignifying their local oral forms. New vantage points emerged as spoken utterances were increasingly captured through audio recordings. Though Goody was not the only influential figure in this congeries of interests, he unquestionably played a central role within it as the 'oral' became increasingly visible and investigated – an object of study in its own right.

Less widely cited but of comparable importance were his substantial field-based publications on the Bagre myth of the West African Lodagaa (northern Ghana). This was recited during the initiation of those opting to join the Bagre association, a society with medical and social benefits for its members. The 'White Bagre' myth was associated with initiation into the first grade and its secrets, the 'Black Bagre' with the second stage:

In the beginning was god,
the god of the initiates,
and their gods ...
(Black Bagre, lines 1–3, in Goody 1972: 224)

Goody's initial view of the lengthy two-part text which he took down from dictation in 1950 was of a myth 'handed down in more or less exact form, as a unique cultural expression, from generation to generation' (2000: 36) – a common enough expectation at the time. Returning later with a tape recorder, he discovered the existence of a multitude – an infinity – of versions. Over several years he and Kum Gandah, a Bagre member, recorded some fifteen versions of the White Bagre and nine of the Black. There were extensive differences between them, noticeable even when the same man recited on different occasions or different people recited on the same occasion (the myth had to be recited three times at each ceremony); those between nearby settlements (ten miles apart, for example) were enormous. The versions varied in content and tone too. In general they revolved round the tripartite relationship of man, God and beings of the wild, but some stressed intermediaries or human agents, others were more theocentric and speculative.

Goody published several analyses of these recitations, significant not only as oral literary forms but also for his concept of 'oral culture': he built on his Bagre experience by consistently emphasizing the variable rather than (as once supposed) fixed nature of oral expression, and the creativity and diversity within a non-literate community. He produced long and meticulously edited texts of several Bagre recitations, complete with translations and detailed commentaries – a massive contribution in itself (Goody 1972, Goody and Gandah 1980). Again, I recall vividly how enlightening I found these, with their empirically as well as analytically based insights and their well-documented revelation of the sophistication with which so-called 'simple' peoples could manipulate their verbal texts and present differing, and sceptical, world views.

So how does Goody characterize 'orality' or the 'oral' in these classic publications which have so expanded the interest in modes of communication? His views, although – or because – they are so widely published and admired, are still subject to much debate.[2] Of equal interest, they contain more than one strand. The second of these, I will argue, deserves far more attention than it has hitherto received.

'Oral', the counterpart of 'written'

The best-known strand in characterizing 'the oral' within Goody's oeuvre has been to counterpose it to 'the written'. This has been a preoccupation throughout his scholarly life, from his 1960s publications to *The*

---

2 The substantial and argumentative literature around Goody's work is a tribute to his influence (any sceptical comments in this book should of course be seen in that light).

Domestication of the Savage Mind (1977), his 1980s 'attempts to spell out some of the general differences between the social organization of societies without and with writing and the process of transition from one to the other' (*Logic of Writing* 1986: xi; also *The Interface between the Written and the Oral* 1987) and his recent volume on 'the nature of the differences between cultures with writing and those without' (Goody 2000: 2; also related comparative works [1996, 1997, 1998]). All are typical Goody productions, marked by both comparative theory and empirical illustration, and returning time after time to the differences between oral and literate societies. Further, 'among the reasons I originally undertook fieldwork in West Africa was the wish to lay out more clearly for myself some features of western society, for example, in the contrast between the written and the oral' (1986: vii). Many have shared Goody's interest, but surely none can match his sustained contribution to the subject through half a century.

Goody's strategy was to explore 'oral culture' through contrast, by considering 'the effects of writing on social organisation and cognitive processes' (Goody 2000: 3). He reveals 'cultures with writing' as characterized by the ability to store and accumulate knowledge, to appeal to and critically examine externally fixed written formulations, engage in formal logic and facilitate bureaucracy – developing 'forms of rationality as well as commerce and social stratification' (1998: 2). 'Oral cultures', he points out, broadly lack these features, except perhaps in 'embryonic' form. Their major focus is on face-to-face relationships with little or no cumulation of knowledge or exact verbal reproduction – thus more flexibility and change, usually unawares in the absence of written records to measure it by. Memory is unsupported by external means, for 'without writing there is virtually no storage of information outside the human brain and hence no communication over great distances and long periods of time' (2000: 27).

What Durkheim saw as the mechanical solidarity of simpler societies is not only a matter of the division of labour. Social relations and values have more obviously to be upheld in face-to-face situations; there is no possible recourse to a text as an external source of guidance ... The restriction of linguistic communication to the oral channel accounts for some of those features that are commonly regarded as characteristic of the 'primitive mentality'. The greater concreteness and relative lack of abstraction must be linked to the dominance of the context of the interactive situation. Inhibitions are placed on the elaboration of general rules, which are more often implicit than explicit. In the terminology developed by Max Weber and Talcott Parsons, such societies tend to be particularistic rather than universalistic.

> Social institutions are much affected by the limitations of the oral channel. Religions tend to have a more local focus, to be more clearly intertwined with everyday life. Legal procedures are less governed by general laws, by formal procedures ... The homeostatic tendencies of

memory usually consign to oblivion what is no longer wanted. Oral communication in the political field obviously restricts the buildup of bureaucratic government. ... The more complex the organization of the state and the economy, the greater the pressure toward the graphic representation of speech. (Goody 2000: 24–5)

At first sight this looks like one of the pervasive narratives of Western cultures: of a radical opposition between primitive and civilized societies/ minds. On the one side, primitive society: uncreative, dominated by religion and magic, homogeneous, communal, local, swayed not by reason but by emotion and custom, 'traditional', non-Western, oral. On the other comes modern culture: progressive, urban, economically developed, civilized and civilizing, secular, scientific, individualistic, heterogeneous, literate, rational. The details of this mighty origin myth have varied over the years – sometimes a story of fixed opposing types, sometimes of a gradual progress up to Western rationality and science – but versions of the story are recycled again and again, through contrasts like simple/complex, modernization/ tradition, development/under-development, ourselves/others. It has seemed to follow that 'orality' is inevitably associated with the first type: unchanging, homogeneous, non-rational.

In fact, though far less often noticed, Goody has been querying certain elements of this myth for a generation, long anticipating the recent challenges to the ethnocentric and loaded features of such 'grand narratives'. He has consistently attacked the assumption that non-literate societies are homogeneous and credulous. In his 1972 edition of the Bagre myth – open-minded and thorough ethnographer that he was – he stressed the existence of scepticism and divergent views within Lodagaa culture. New initiates were positively encouraged to go round different Bagre performances and learn from them (2000: 126) and there were multiple differing versions of the myth (the kind of differences, he comments, often overlooked by lazy ethnographers [1998: 220]). He finds 'scepticism widespread in oral cultures' (1998: 184), and rebuts the stereotype of oral cultures as unchanging and uncreative, questioning the 'communal memory' once widely assumed to distinguish 'primitive' society from the individualism of literate modernity (2000: 43–4). He also queries the once-prevalent view that 'orality' is now outdated and superseded by writing – the simplistic version of unilinear evolutionism – for it remains a dominant form of human interaction, even if modified 'by the addition of new means and modes of communication' (2000: 2).

Goody similarly rejects the notion that the advent of 'literacy' had automatic and immediate results. He initially spoke of its 'consequences' (Goody and Watts 1963/68) but later preferred to speak of 'implications' and multiple changes rather than monocausal determinism. There was *not*, he says, some wholesale transformation of society after the invention of writing, but a gradual process interacting with other developments: 'in

taking writing and the written tradition as my topic ... I do not imply
for one moment that these are the only factors involved in any specific
situation, only that they are significant ones' (Goody 1986: xv). Rather than
a sharp discontinuity between radically opposed types of society, elements
that were already implicit became fully developed in 'written cultures', for
writing made explicit 'processes [which] are embryonically present in oral
societies' (1996: 242; also 1997: 16).

Above all, he goes out of his way to challenge both the 'great divide'
tradition which sets a definitive chasm between ourselves and our prede-
cessors, and the over-privileging of European experience that this so often
implies. Witness his clarion call introducing *The Myth of the Bagre*.

> Even anthropological readers are only too ready to assume a great divide
> between 'primitive' and 'civilized' thought, between 'mythopoeic' and
> 'logico-empirical' modes, between the wild and domesticated varieties ...
> It is a view that requires a major revision ... The radical dichotomy that
> lies at the basis of such sociological and anthropological thinking, as well
> as behind popular belief itself, seems to me entirely unacceptable, a relic
> of academic colonialism. (Goody 1972: 3; also 1986: 181–2).

Goody's own approach is to focus on more specific investigations,
exploring the cognitive processes and social institutions linked to modes
of communication and analysing them within a developmental framework.
This means rejecting elements of the generalized discontinuity versions of
the traditional myth. His ethnographically informed approach brings out
instead continuities and gradual transitions associated with changes in
communication. The overall development, both social and cognitive, was in
one general direction, but the advance was complex and uneven (1977: 151).

> The balance of my argument continues to be a delicate one. In the first
> place, I have attempted to set aside radical dichotomies; in the second, I
> reject diffuse relativism. The third course involves a more difficult task,
> that of specifying particular mechanisms ... [analysing] some aspects of the
> processes of communication in order to try to elucidate what others have
> tried to explain by means of those dichotomies. This is not a great-divide
> theory. It sees some changes as more important than others, but it attempts
> to relate specific differences to specific changes. (Goody 1977: 50).

All the same, Goody's long insistence on the contrasts between oral and
written cultures carries echoes of the Western origin myth. He seems to
accept the notion of a contrast between societal types ('traditional'/'modern',
'simple'/'complex', 'primitive'/'advanced') as a self-evident issue that needs
further – though of course more self-critical – explanation (e.g. 1977: 50,
1995: 138, 2000: 8). This is his point of departure for examining the specific
mechanisms bringing about these differences and for his own alternative

explication of the differences between simple and civilized cultures. Despite his qualifications, these are credited above all to the advent of literacy: 'writing allowed a quantum jump in human consciousness, in cognitive awareness'(1998: 1). His magisterial *The Power of the Written Tradition* treats the nature of the differences between cultures with writing and those without: 'the line of argument and the presentation of evidence develop a theme that I and others have previously proposed, stressing the transforming effects of literate activity on human life (2000: 2). The message is that 'the emergence of writing and literate activity some five thousand years ago transformed human life as profoundly as the earlier revolution of intensive agriculture' (2000: blurb).

Goody links his own typology of oral versus literate societies with those of earlier theorists like Durkheim, Weber and Parsons and with distinctions such as those posited between 'simple' and 'complex' societies, 'domesticated' and 'savage', 'primitive' and 'advanced', 'hot' and 'cold' (e.g. 1977: 16, 147, 2000: 5, 1987: 290–1; also 2000: 24–5, quoted above). Indeed one element in the welcome accorded to his work may partly lie in the resonances that some readers find, rightly or wrongly, with these still deeply emotive classifications.

Goody's delineation of 'oral' through its contrast with written eventually turns out to be somewhat elusive. This is partly because he in fact focuses more fully and directly on the implications of *written* than of oral communication. In sketching the nature of 'oral cultures' he does make some direct points about flexibility, creativity and change; cultural homeostasis; the relative insignificance of material mechanisms for cumulating knowledge or communicating across space and time (a debatable point); the possibility of scepticism and diverse views; and the shadowy existence of 'embryonic' forms to be more fully developed in 'civilized cultures'.

Are we then to conclude that these are characteristics of all truly 'oral cultures'? That they regularly go together and are (or were?) therefore likely to be further associated with, for example, localized outlook, relative lack of bureaucracy, low division of labour, little explicit rationality or abstraction, particularistic rather than universalistic norms? And, as sometimes implied in Goody's terminology, that all this together constitutes 'oral culture' as a type about which we can generalize – a better-informed version of the traditional myth, then, this time depicting not a grand fixed chasm but a gradual transition from one pole to the other, with some quantum leaps and major transformations on the way, leading ultimately to the literate culture of the modern West?

Or, rather, are these traits which are often – but not always – found in specific cases of oral communication, which can therefore best be examined as specific, relative and varying processes in particular historical contexts? That would fit with some of Goody's exposition. But if so, are some features more salient than others and where does this leave the characterization of 'orality' or 'oral culture'? Just as it is now recognized that it is not so much a matter of 'literacy' as of multiple literacies, so too there are no doubt multiple oralities, a huge diversity of ways in which humans turn oral communicating to their uses. Amid this, has the 'oral' perhaps dissolved as something in its own right? At any rate, within Goody's strategy of revealing it as the counterpart of 'written', the exact conclusions about the 'oral' end of the oral–literate juxtaposition remain somewhat cloudy.

A further difficulty is the focus on the oral–literate contrast itself. This has the advantage, admittedly, of replacing wholesale generalization about 'primitive society' (etc.) by specific investigations concerning speech and writing. But such a choice is also to narrow down on one model of humanity: privileging language as *the* key dimension of human history and culture.

This is in tune with the long-entrenched view of humanity in Western tradition discussed earlier, one that received particular impetus in Enlightenment formulations. In its essentials, this ideology of language as humankind's defining characteristic is still highly influential today. It often reiterates Astle's eighteenth-century assertion that 'without *speech* we should scarcely have been rational beings' (1784: 2) and that the invention of writing 'hath contributed more than all others to the improvement of mankind' (1784: 10). This is often enough extended into an account, overlapping with elements of both the divide and the developmental narrative, which depicts the rational functions of language as not only setting humanity apart from animals but, through the advent of writing (above all in its full alphabetic form), moving humanity onward into the scientific efflorescence of the West.

Goody presses the same paradigm. Language is the overriding constituent of human culture whose presence over the ages may even have altered human physiology through 'the enlargement of the right hemisphere of the brain' (Goody 2000: 133). And:

> the most significant elements of any human culture are undoubtedly channelled through words, and reside in the particular range of meanings and attitudes which members of any society attach to their verbal symbols. (Goody and Watt 1968: 28)

Later too, 'the acquisition of language, which is an attribute of mankind alone, is basic to all social institutions, to all normative behaviour' (Goody 1977: 9).

Goody is thus another exponent of the Western myth delineated in Chapter 2: language is the specific human attribute, the critical means of interaction between individuals, the foundation of the development of what we call 'culture' and of the way in which learned behaviour is transmitted from one generation to the next. But if language is inextricably associated with 'culture', it is writing that is linked with 'civilization', with the culture of cities, with complex social formations (1987: 3). 'In societies without writing', he writes', 'the spoken form of language – oral communication – bears all the burden of cultural transmission' (2000: 23). Then comes writing to transcribe speech into visual form, with 'effects ... on social organization and cognitive processes ... of primary importance in the history of human cultures' (2000: 3–4); 'cognitively as well as sociologically, writing underpins "civilization"' (1987: 300). Or again, differences such as those between primitive and advanced 'can reasonably be attributed to the advent of writing and the subsequent developments – the formalization of discourse, the extension of some forms of abstraction, of logic (e.g. the syllogism) and of rationality' (1987: 291).

From this perspective, then, the key factor in human development is verbal language and the two forms (spoken and transcribed) in which this is handled. These are crucial not just for social organization but for cognitive development too, manifested in technologies of the 'intellect', storage of knowledge, the 'mentalities' related to changes from oral to literate communication, and (in time) the formalized rational dimensions of writing. The differences are set 'in a developmental way' (Goody 1995: 137) along a linguistically based continuum, culminating finally in the 'full' form of alphabetic writing (1999: 30). This is not so far from the outlook of intellectuals such as Thomas Astle. It fits well into a cognitive, language-centred model of the nature and destiny of humanity which has been one powerful theme within Western thought – but one not necessarily shared by all cultural traditions. Of lesser importance in this paradigm – indeed tacitly swept aside – are the pictorial, sculptural, gestural, tactile, musical, choreographic, affective or artefactual dimensions of human life.

And yet, other aspects of Goody's work seem to tell a different story. He, of all anthropologists, has set the role of language in human affairs into perspective by complementing his studies of the oral and literate with striking accounts of other dimensions of human culture. These necessarily – if only implicitly – convey the insufficiency of a linguistically defined model of humanity. This breadth is clearly evident in his detailed ethnographic analyses, while his comparative works on food and cooking, the culture of flowers, love, iconography and image (Goody 1982, 1993, 1996, 1997, 1998) take us well beyond any assumption that words are everything or that the features embraced in the literate/oral contrast make up the whole of culture. He considers 'visual mnemonics' like the Australian Aboriginal stylized maps formulated in their sacred *tchuringa*, the insignia of the Ashanti 'golden stool', or the Native American Ojibway birch-bark drawings (Goody 2000: 30–2), his *Representations and Contradictions* (1997) ranges generously over painting, sculpture, visual images, theatre and relics, while more recently (2012) he has turned to the significance of metal in human history.

This vein in Goody's work suggests a very different viewpoint on the 'oral'. So rather than pursuing the more general oral/literate comparisons for which he is so famous, I propose now to follow up this second strand.

Putting the 'oral' in context

To do so, we can return to Goody's accounts of the Bagre. His 1972 version of the White Bagre opens with one of the 'first' two men (the 'elder') consulting a diviner about the causes of humanity's recurrent ills:

> *Gods,*
> *ancestors,*
> *guardians,*
> *beings of the wild,*
> *the leather bottles*
> *say we should perform,*
> *because of the scorpion's sting,*
> *because of suicide,*
> *aches in the belly,*
> *pains in the head.*
> *The elder brother*
> *Slept badly.*
> *He took out some guinea corn*
> *And hurried along*
> *To the diviner ...*
> *And he picked up 'deity'*
> *And he picked up 'the wild'*
> *And he picked up 'sacrifice'.*
> *He picked up 'deity',*
> *That was what*
> *He picked up first.*
> *He picked out 'deity'*
> *And began to ask,*
> *What 'deity'?*
> (lines 1–15, 20–7, Goody 1972: 121)

The speaker is then led to the deity of 'meetings', among which the Bagre initiation rites are among the most important. The text continues (from line 60) with words which go along with the ritual and are recited during it, explaining and prescribing the ceremonies as they are performed.

On the face of it, what we have here is a verbal text. In the major publications of the myth (Goody 1972, Goody and Gandah 1980), it is the one-lined text that is printed and translated and the notes focus on the words and their meaning. The myth is to be defined, it appears, by its transcribed words. The verbal elaboration is in fact impressive. The dictated version of the White Bagre runs to over 6,000 lines (78 pages in its double-column translation in Goody 1972), and others too stretch to several thousand lines. But when we look closer, it becomes clear from

Goody's account that the verbal text we see in the printed book was emphatically not the full action.[3]

Goody shows that the recitation is marked not just by speech but by non-verbal components and their settings. The White Bagre recitations are performances rather than self-standing verbal texts, performances furthermore that are inextricably enmeshed into the enactment of a prolonged series of ceremonies and interwoven with music, dance and sociability.

Probably the most talked-about and rejoiced-in part of social life is the series of Bagre performances, associated with 'the deity of meetings', of coming together. For here, in the long, warm evenings, there is the music of the xylophones, the poetry of the myth, the dancing of the young, the conversation of the old, and plenty of beer, food and girls (Goody 1972: 12). Many of the participants were themselves initiates from previous occasions and for them in particular, 'the performance of the ceremonies themselves, the food, the beer, the music, the throng of dancers, the subjection of the neophytes to ordeals through which one has successfully passed – all is a source of pleasure to the initiated' (1972: 41). And for all 'it is a time of relaxation and enjoyment' (1972: 41).

If that is the framework, what about the utterances themselves? Goody gives us some indications of the modes of delivery. The ritual sections delivered by the senior reciters were in a special 'recitativo' form, delivered rapidly to a beaten accompaniment. Each phrase was echoed by those present and repeated three times. Its *manner* of recitation, different from that for any other Lodagaa verbal genre, was part of its message and meaning. There were also relatively discrete prayers or songs where the initiands and others were singing, chanting or 'crying out' in prayer. The final dance involved large numbers of people with joint singing, some of it no doubt in the classic African 'call and response' mode, together with xylophone players and drummers. The varying styles of delivery brought their own contribution to people's experience and understanding, well beyond the impression given by the printed words alone.

Music, song, rhythm and instrumental accompaniment were part of these performances. A rhythmic beat was essential. A reciter shook a rattle, tapped on a shrine, or was accompanied by beats on xylophone slats; other participants too produced rhythms whether by a sacrificial knife, a stone struck on an altar, sticks on wood, or tapping a calabash. The rhythm of

---

3　The analysis in this section is based on Goody 1972, 1987: esp. 167ff., 1997: Ch. 5, 2000: esp. 36ff., 49ff., Goody and Gandah 1980, also shorter dispersed comments elsewhere in Goody's publications. My discussion is selective, with no attempt to give a full account of the lengthy and elaborate ceremonies involved (for which see references above). The analysis mainly refers to the White Bagre, of whose performance Goody has given much fuller descriptions, but it seems that the less ritual-based Black Bagre too had musical, rhythmic, visual, proxemic and artefactual dimensions.

the Black Bagre – faster and more complex than the White – was beaten out
by xylophone sticks on a wooden plank or trough. The large-scale dancing
at the climax of the ceremony was enlivened by drums, xylophones and
song. Other sounds too sometimes formed part of the performance: hand
clapping, iron bells, ululation, and gun shots when the neophytes emerged
from their room after successfully passing their ordeals.

The one-voice impression given by the linear printed text does not match
the reality. There is some basis for it, for much of the formal recitation
was in one sense delivered by single individuals. But in practice multiple
participants took part at different points in the ceremony: leaders, elders,
guides, relatives, second-graders, the initiands themselves and, at some
points, the gathered crowd of spectators. The leading part was taken by
one or more 'speakers', senior men who carried out the main recitation,
instructing the neophytes who sat patiently to listen to them in the secluded
Bagre room in which they spent much of their time. These sections were
performed three times over (sometimes by two people reciting simultaneously, to save time!), up to the point when a particular ceremony was to
begin, providing both a kind of mnemonic and an explanation of it. The
initiands chanted too, repeating the speakers' words. Other phases were in
the open air, where the leader's chant could be taken up line by line by the
whole assembly as the participants as a whole – spectators and supporters
as well as initiands – gathered together in the specified locations. At certain
stages the neophytes had to sing as they went about their ceremonial tasks,
for example circling three times to find their hidden ritual bells, and songs
were sung by their sponsors or guides; sometimes new songs were created
about them for playing outside the Bagre room.

The voices of *several* reciters could thus overlap and intertwine simultaneously, sometimes interspersed with comments or corrections from
experienced listeners or mixed with shouts or ululations from the gathered
participants. It is not self-evident where – or whether – one should draw
a line between the text 'proper' and contingent 'interruptions': in a sense
all were part of the performance as actually produced and experienced.
The whole atmosphere and setting with its interactive engagement of many
participants besides the 'lead' reciters helped to shape its meaning.

The result of all this is that the words-as-transcribed are far from
conveying all the auditory features. Even less do they communicate the
visual dimensions of the performance. Goody depicts the White Bagre as
both 'visual and verbal action ... tied to ritual, to a set of standardized
visual acts' (1987: 171). As well as the observed ceremonial enactments
without which the Bagre recitation could not be properly accomplished at
all, the speakers' gestures helped to structure the chant, the reciter of the
moment raising and lowering his left arm 'to mark the beginning and the
end of formal speech, during which period no interruption will be possible'
(2000: 53). The initiands' visible appearance was another carefully managed
feature of the whole. At various stages they had to don special clothing,

carry prescribed objects, and have their hair shaved or dressed in special ways and their bodies whitewashed with thick white stripes. At the end they processed in public in their finery, displaying their Bagre accoutrements and visibly supported by their sponsors and admirers.

The spatial arrangements were also part of the occasion: where people were positioned, their respective spacing, how they were marshalled. The initiates took up particular locations for the different stages, spending much of it in their special room listening to the recitation of relevant parts of the Bagre myth but emerging to enact ceremonies in prescribed places, be led in procession or assembled in due order. People's movements were relevant too, embodied experience as well as visual display. The neophytes had to conduct themselves in particular ways, showing their status not just through their words but in their bearing: downcast eyes and silent humble demeanour, thrown off only when their induction was complete. Other actions too, such as using oil to create relationships between ancestors and initiands, beating the shrines, running 'elegantly' – all were necessary dimensions of the full enactment. So too was food and drink. Commensalism and fasting were parts of the unfolding ceremonies, and the neophytes' avoidance and consumption of food and beer at the due points constituted public declarations of commitment validating the ceremonial sequence.

The movements of dance were particularly prominent. 'The xylophones begin to play and all present, both men and women, join in the Bagre dance … the girls gather round in a circle at the side and dance and sing to the clapping of hands' (Goody 1972: 75). The culmination of the ritual was the 'Bagre Dance' when the new members were formally inducted into the society. It took place over three days, often when the moon was full to light up the complex scene. The whole was brilliant with singing and instrumental music – especially xylophones and drums, whose histories and donors were part of the whole – as well as food, beer and the ambience of courtship and play.

In the published texts the words are brought together as 'the myth'. But in practice they were enacted in a series of performances as the initiation ritual unfolded over several months, and were performed by several different participants at different times. The whole was united less as verbal text – the impression given by its identity in print – than as protracted series of linked enactments.

Une unité comme celle le Bagré possède ne repose pas sur la seule narration verbale. En vérité, on ne peut considérer la récitation que comme partie de l'ensemble total qu'est la célébration, la cérémonie (et, dans ce sens, le rite). (Goody and Gandah 1980: 52)

A unity like the Bagre's does not just lie in its verbal performance. In fact one can only regard the recitation as part of a totality, made up of the celebration, the ceremony (and, in this sense, the ritual). [Author's translation]

So – sounds of many kinds, modes of delivery, visual gesture and spacing, clothing and material accoutrements, bodily adornment, demeanour, movement, dance, food, drink, sociability, pride, excitement, emotion: all these were not 'mere' context but integral to the meanings and experiences of the Bagre performances. Goody conveys it well in another context when he comments on 'the immediacy of the face-to-face contact, the visual gesture and tones of voice [marking] oral communication. It is the play seen, the symphony heard, rather than the drama read, the score studied' (Goody 1977: 50).

This strand in Goody's treatment brings out the multidimensionality of oral expression, giving a richer and more contextually based approach to characterizing the oral. Not all cases will be just like the Bagre, of course, but Goody's account gives us a clue to the kind of range that can be looked for when we encounter the term 'oral'. Orality is revealed as multiplex rather than a matter of words alone.[4] Many dimensions can enter in: visual, kinesic, acoustic (not just the verbal sounds but other sonic effects too), proxemic, material, tactile, bodily presence and movement – all are potentially relevant, if to varying degrees depending on occasion, participants and location. This approach provides a more rounded and more realistic viewpoint on what is involved in oral expression than the thinner, linguistically based model.

Perspectives on language, speech and writing

The multimodal and contextual approach to oral expression and communication in this strand of Goody's work chimes with several other transdisciplinary developments, in particular changing attitudes to the analysis of language. Where the emphasis used to be on decontextualized and impersonal properties and on textual products, recent analyses now increasingly take on the idea of language as action. Some of these streams date back some time, like Goffman's dramatistic approaches, Austin's 'speech acts', and work in the ethnography of speaking, performance and experience by anthropologists and sociolinguists. But they are now flowing together into a view of speech and communication not as autonomous systems of signs for conveying independent pieces of information but modes of social action, created by interacting human agents in specific situations.[5]

The spotlight is thus turned on people's actions rather than on self-standing systems of signs, and on people's active deployment of a wealth of

---

4 The same could be said of the comparable, though not identical, multimodality of writing, a topic it is not possible to pursue here (for some comment see Finnegan 2002: 229ff.).
5 On these developments see for example Clark 1992, Duranti 1997, 2001, Hanks 1996, Tracey 1999.

varied resources. Verbal language in the narrow sense is indeed one of these, and an important one – but only one. In their communicating, humans also regularly exploit such diverse tools as facial expression, gesture, bodily orientation, spatial indications, movement, touch, images, and a variegated range of material objects, from sceptres, flags or guns to meaningful apparel, stethoscopes and pulpits.

Even if we focus only on the auditory dimensions of speech, we have to take account of intonation, tempo, dialect, rhythm, volume, timbre, emphasis and all the near-infinite modulations of the speaking – and singing – voice. These may not appear in the traditional grammar books, but they are essential for language-in-use – a huge constellation of potential resources for communication and expression.

This also connects with recent debates about the language–rationality association – the viewpoint, that is, that was conveyed in Astle's presentation of speech as enabling men to be rational, and formulated most directly in Locke's prescriptive, 'scientific' and referential view of language. Despite its pervasive influence, however, this is actually only one view of language and of humanity.

A counter-tradition is now making a comeback. Language is starting to be seen as contextual, multisensory, emotive and intertextual (see Bauman and Briggs 2000). Linguistic anthropologists and 'social interaction' linguists, among others, are highlighting the multidimensional features of linguistic action, and the emotional as well as the cognitive aspects of language. Some argue for a wider definition of 'language' to encompass the gestures coordinated with speech (Haviland 2001, McNeill 2000, Sheldon 1999, Streeck and Knapp 1992) or see 'context' as integral to linguistic action (Duranti and Goodwin 1992), undermining any supposition that the *settings* of performances like the Bagre are only peripheral. The multisensory dimensions, together with the audiences, spacings, sounds, gestures, accoutrements, touches and so on, are not 'merely contingent' when set against the ostensibly more concrete conceptualizations within the verbal text, but themselves a solid part of the action.

This broader outlook gains further support from yet other threads in recent scholarship. A sensitivity to the manifold dimensions of our human experience is scarcely new, but recent approaches to material culture, cultural history, studies of the body and its adornment, and the anthropology of the senses have all been highlighting the complex spectrum of multisensory and multimedia resources used in human communication, our use of 'mediational' forms of communicating as well as our somatic interactions.[6] Scholars across several disciplines are challenging the assumption

---

6 See for example Graves-Brown 2000, Kwint et al. 1999, Schiffer 1999, Burke 1997, Entwhistle 2000, Featherstone 2000, Classen 1997, Howes 1991, Scollon 1999, Silverstone 1999.

that human life and communication is fully described by its cognitive features, just as studies of language are taking on affective as well as conceptual aspects. Human beings are not solely intellectual or linguistic creatures, and their pictures, gestures, costumes, facial expressions, human-made artefacts or bodily movements are also significant dimensions of their communicating.

Work in performance studies feeds into this too. From informal conversations or everyday greetings to more heightened and formalized art forms, their import cannot be appreciated through the words alone without some consideration of, for example, visual effects, music, material accoutrements such as dress, audience interaction, or location. As the ethnomusicologist Ruth Stone has so well demonstrated, epic performances in Liberia are not just heard, far less satisfactorily represented in written transcriptions for they are seen, heard and *felt* by their audience-participants in all the dramatic intermingling of instrumentation, song, narrative, vivid gesturing, and dance. The epic here is not a purely textual entity but an aural, kinetic, visual and choreographic event: a performance by particular actors in a specific – enchanted – moment of time and space (Stone 1998: 135ff.). Across a range of disciplines like linguistic anthropology, folklore, performance studies, ethnomusicology and sociolinguistics it is now accepted practice to inquire into the multi-dimensionality of performance.

The technology of writing naturally privileges the ontological status of the written word. Dictated texts like Goody's first Bagre version once seemed to give the 'real thing': the single-voiced linear text, fixed and recorded through writing. But the widening availability of audio technology has revealed new facets, strikingly exemplified in Parry and Lord's discoveries about the mingled variability and formulaic qualities of Yugoslav sung epic (Lord 1960) as well as in Goody's later audio recordings of the Bagre performances and in the extensive work on the sonic features of oral expression, from African story-telling to Native American verbal art and beyond. We can hear and analyse volume, tempo, dynamics, intonation, intensity, participating audiences, song, all capturable on audiotape. And now video can record gesture, visual display, material symbols, spacing and dance, supplementing still photography by the experience of movement, temporal development and the seen dynamics of audience and performer interactions. Study of *all* the participants – not just the apparent 'lead' performer – is encouraged by the advantage of audiovisual technology over print for capturing multiple voices. The Bagre dancers and their actions, the xylophone players, the responding choruses, the massed procession – all are part of the Bagre, not just the senior 'speakers' whose words appear in the published transcripts. Inevitably our awareness of what is involved in oral expression – even what an oral form really 'is' – has been widened from a prime focus on writable one-voice texts towards an appreciation of the multifacetedness of oral performance.

This brings us back to the relation of writing to speaking, an issue which needs some further comment. Earlier scholars often regarded writing as essentially a transcript of speech and thus most fully developed in the phonologically based alphabetic system. This tends to be Goody's approach too, complementing his view of the centrality of the two modes for handling language, humankind's key attribute: speech and its transcript in writing. Writing is the 'means of recording speech ... [the] visual transcription of oral linguistic elements' (1987: 54, 78). Alphabetic scripts are the 'fully fledged writing systems with which one can transcribe the whole range of the spoken word' (Goody 1999: 30).

This model is now under attack from several directions however, as both lacking comparative perspective and out of touch with current realities. In fact, not all writing systems are parasitic on spoken language nor directly representative of it (unless, that is, one takes the narrowest of definitions by which *only* alphabetic scripts can qualify as 'true' writing). Some recent analysts argue convincingly that such examples as Chinese writing or Mesoamerican pictorial and hieroglyphic systems can be described as 'semasiographic' in that, in contrast to phonographic systems, the visible marks 'communicate meaning directly ... independently from language' (Boone and Mignolo in their aptly titled *Writing Without Words*, 1994: 15); here the meaning is *not* ultimately reducible to, nor a transcription of, spoken words.[7] It was once widely taken for granted that such forms were either dead ends or, at best, merely evolutionary antecedents on the way to 'full writing' as manifested in the alphabet – 'the most highly developed, the most convenient and the most easily adaptable system of writing ... now universally employed by civilized peoples' (Diringer 1968, vol. 1: 13).

Given the variety of visual-graphic communication systems that might be encompassed in broad definitions of 'writing', it is surely a limited ethnocentric view which assumes alphabetic systems as unquestionably the pinnacle of writing's development. Though alphabetic writing has indeed ousted other forms as part of imperialist Western expansion, it does not follow that non-speech-based systems are in themselves less efficient, subtle or 'contemporary'. Chinese writing is used by a sizeable proportion of the world's population, based largely (though not wholly) on 'stylised drawings of things in combination with one another to convey ideas' (Brown 1998: 17); it shares with other semasiographic systems – among them musical and mathematical notations – the advantage of transcending linguistic barriers. In fact even in 'alphabetic' systems, a significant role is played by non-phonetic elements: images, diagrams, numbers, layout, spatial

---

7 Terminologies for writing systems – even the delimitation of 'writing' itself – of course remain controversial. For some provocative and insightful recent accounts see Biddle 2002, Boone and Mignolo 1994, Harris 2000, Kress 2002, Perri 2001.

relationships, typography etc.[8] (this often remains unrecognized in folk ideologies which envisage writing as the mirror of speech). Non-verbal visual presentations, furthermore, are central in modern science and our prolific contemporary usage of images, icons, and computer-mediated visual display is being further enhanced by technologies for transferring images across space through faxing, scanning and the web.

This joins with the transdisciplinary developments mentioned earlier to challenge and enlarge the word-based model of both writing and human culture more generally. Linguistically based forms, it turns out, are far from the only modes of communication. Besides the visual images so important today, there are and have been multiple other modes and media throughout the world: the classic forms of dance and mime, both Western and non-Western; silent films and cartoons; the complex gestural systems of some Native American or Australian peoples or the comparable British Sign Language used so effectively by deaf people to communicate in three-dimensional space; the Walbiri/Warlpiri 'sand stories' and 'trace' inscribing of aboriginal Australia; the miniature brass images representing proverbs once used to weigh gold in West Africa; the pictorial narratives on cathedral façades or stained-glass windows; South Pacific 'story boards'; and the many other 'material memories' which are indeed used in communicating but which it would surely be far-fetched to regard as transcriptions of speech.[9]

The 'oral–literate' continuum is starting to look incomplete as a compass for human modes of communication. Nor are interactions between different modes exhaustively described by considering the apparent opposites of oral and written. The colonial period of Aztec Mexico, for instance, saw a triadic relationship between oral communication, Latin alphabet and local pictographic writing (Perri 2001: 273), while in parts of Africa the communicative modes of drums, dance, song, displays of clothing or three-dimensional wooden or metal images contended, complemented and mingled with spoken word or written scripts. Modes of communication are more multisided than can be conveyed by word-based models, for humans draw variously and disparately on a multiplex spectrum of sounded words, graphic representations, music, gestures, images – and much more.

These various perspectives are replacing a view of human culture as based primarily on verbal language – oral and written – with more

---

8   Also recognized by Goody, e.g. in his discussion of numerals and of 'graphic representation [such as] ... the table ... the matrix ...' (Goody 1986: xiii) and his criticism of simplistic 'visible speech' models (1977: 76, 124). But he keeps returning to language as the bedrock: such tables are the 'graphic representation of language' (1986: xiii), writing is 'the graphic representation of speech' (2000: 25), and the mnemonic images described in Frances Yates's study of memory involve 'the prior reduction of language to a visual form' (Goody 1985: 16).

9   For elaboration and references see Finnegan 2002, also Biddle 2002, Kwint et al. 1999, Perri 2001, Rumsey 2001.

complicated models embracing a multiplicity of media and resources. Goody's term of 'technology' can similarly be enlarged, from just ways of handling language to other communicative modes too: to the diverse cultural systems surrounding the uses of pictures and images, of buildings and costume, of dance, of touch and space, and of the formalized usages of bodily movement in gesture – 'this old, efficient, and beautiful technology of communication' (Streeck 1994: 266).

The perspective in Goody's work that widens the conspectus beyond a narrow focus on words is thus both supported and further extended by current perspectives on the multiplicity of communicating. This in turn entails questioning the powerful but arguably ethnocentric model which picks out the verbal as the key element whether in any given act of communicating or in the long development of human culture and communication more generally which also lies among Goody's interests.

The 'oral' – dissolved or reclad?

Should we then give up the term 'oral'? It has lost its pre-eminent position as one of *the* two crucial poles in the (linguistic) framework shaping human cognitive and social processes, for insofar as it is a distinguishable term at all it is only one of several communicative technologies. Neither is it a clear-cut concept with self-evident edges, but constantly entangled with other modes and media. It only too easily carries a loaded set of connotations with it also. Especially when used as a key term for analysing human cultures or history in some general sense, it so often seems irretrievably intershot with questionable overtones of uniformity, of verbal prioritizing or even, at times, of the ethnocentric origin myth-telling of either radical dichotomy or a progressive development up to Western-oriented forms.

There is something to be said for keeping 'oral' as a limited analytic term, however. If human communication is indeed multimodal and multimedia, it is helpful to sort out the variegated threads even if they *are* in practice intertwined. Even though more elusive and multiplex than used to be supposed, vocal speech *is* still clearly one important dimension of human communication. So it can be illuminating to explore the diverse ways that differing aspects of vocal utterances can be co-created in conjunction with (for example) written overtones, visual images, auditory resonances, musical enactments, material artefacts, bodily engagements. Unpicking the oral features and how they are brought into play enables a fuller appreciation of the complexity of communicating.

There are two corollaries to this. First, the term has many ambiguities, not least that between 1) what is spoken, uttered through the mouth and 2) everything that is not written (the first thus excluding physical monuments, gestural systems or instrumental music, the second including them). The former is arguably more useful, but whichever coverage is intended this certainly needs to be made clear – a simple-sounding injunction, but by no means always observed in scholarly discussion as one sense seeps into another and 'oral' is deployed ambiguously as if its meaning is self-evident. Second, if 'oral' is used in this potentially more delimited sense, where are its boundaries? 'Uttered through the mouth' or 'vocalized' appears precise, a good focus for investigation and analysis.

But of course, as soon as we start digging the edges start dissolving. Is it just the 'words', in the sense of units transcribable into writing? Or also pauses, intensities or volume – elements that in writing might be partially signalled by punctuation or layout? What about sobs, laughs, silences? Or the indications of mood, irony or emotion that can come through in intonation or dynamics, or the multi-level meanings wound into the overlapping of several voices? It seems scarcely possible to omit such elements (or indeed to sideline them by marginalizing terms like 'paralinguistic'). But if so, can we exclude the gestures, facial expressions, spacings, that can play a comparable part in shaping meanings? And what of the visible and palpable accoutrements that sometimes go along with these: the recorded or broadcast vocal sounds that are nowadays a significant dimension of contemporary culture, or the instrumental sounds and sonic ambiences that mediate and formulate their impact? Further, the immediacy of the unrolling event, the temporal moment of performance, the overlapping involvement of the co-participants' bodily presences – all these too may, and probably will, have their own creative input and shape the emergence of potentially multiple meanings in ways that would be seriously undervalued by an analysis of spoken 'words' alone. Again the oral, even in the apparently limited sense of vocalized utterances, turns out to have permeable boundaries indeed.

Taking 'oral' as a focus, then, demands an awareness of its lack of clear delimitation, the need for greater clarity as to *which* potentially multiplex elements are included, and an awareness of the arbitrary and perhaps culture-bound nature of the boundaries we set, likely to vary with situation and folk definition as well as with the analyst's interests. All in all this can only throw further doubt on general conclusions about the 'oral' as a basis for social organization or mental processes even as it alerts us to its complexity and multidimensionality.

Perhaps in the end we need to look at 'oral' not as a settled descriptive or analytic term after all, but as a prompt to explore a range of questions. It is true that for something to be reasonably termed 'oral' at all we would (probably) expect some aspect of voice to be somehow involved; but this can only be the starting point for a series of questions about the range of dimensions and media with which it might be interwoven: visual, auditory, tactile, kinesic, proxemic, material, musical resonances, pictorial associations, evocations of written words (that too), somatic presences and movements. In practice, most forms labelled 'oral' turn out to have some element of multidimensionality about them. To illuminate this fully, a host of issues are there to be pursued: the local conventions and institutions which to an extent formulate, facilitate and constrain the intermixtures; folk ideologies about the ideal or actual mixtures and their relative significance; how people manipulate or extend or, perhaps, narrow down the relatively accepted spectrum on particular occasions or with particular participants. It is only an openness to exploring the range across this kind of broad multisensory and multimedia spectrum that can really give us insight into the oral.

This perspective draws attention to the multifaceted sophistication of human modes of communication. To make expression through words, the key factor is to rest content with a much feebler vision. We would do better to follow and extend Goody's insights into the multiplexity of the Bagre oral performances and of the iconography, material monuments, ritual actions, scents and sights on which he has written so eloquently.

Paradoxically this leads back into a challenge to those very word-based models of human development and experience which he also promotes, linked to a linguistic concept of human culture along the 'orality–literacy' scale. It is timely to reassert that second strand of his work to open a broader perspective on the 'oral' – reclothing it within the rich complexity which has too often been overlooked.

6

Song. What comes first: words, music, or performance?

This chapter follows up the earlier discussions and examples but this time brings in music (crucial human art, so closely connected – and so often overlooked – with the verbal) and concludes that the issues are more complex than just ending up in a satisfied way with 'performance'. All three are commonly necessary aspects of song (and, in a way, of all art-ful speech) that are seldom confronted together. Their respective weight varies not only between cultures, languages and genres, but also among individual artists and occasions, as exemplified in this chapter where my interest in music as well as literature has proved very relevant.

So – which comes first? In the African oral literature I have studied, vocal music is commonly prominent; or, to put it another way, sung and chanted words. This is hardly unique to that continent for it is found throughout the world, realized in a broad and variegated range of genres from Western high art (Bach cantatas, Schubert *Lieder*, Puccini opera) or medieval ecclesiastical chant to popular dance songs, wept lamentations, declaimed epics, songs in Indian films, magical incantations, rock vocals, favourite hymns, intoned sermons or the songs of urchins on the streets. It overlaps into 'poetry', above all what has been called 'oral poetry'. It includes singing, chanting, declaiming, recitative, cantillating, from solemn sacred recitation to the commercial jingles of urban marketing.

'Song' (as I might call it in shorthand reference to that large span of human artistry): in some form or another it is certainly so widespread throughout human times and cultures as surely to count as one of the true universals of our human life. Sometimes the preserve of specialists or supported by elaborate instrumental sounds and complicated technologies, it also in a sense falls within the experience of everyone. Ultimately we need only the sounding voice and the hearing ear.

In some ways then it seems the simplest and most fundamental of the arts. And yet it is also among the most subtle and cultivated of human practices. There is something special about *sung* words. They are removed somehow from the ordinary, somehow distanced from and transcending the present, standing out as art and performance. And even the apparently simplest of songs is wonderfully complex, with words, music and performance somehow remarkably coming together.

What is song?

How can we approach this amazingly complex and intricate phenomenon of song – of vocal music, sung literature? I want to focus down on certain issues that arise when we take seriously the question of how we bind together the three dimensions of words, music, performance. The three are often considered separately, the more so that scholars have approached them from different angles, coming from their own disciplinary perspectives. But it can be an illuminating challenge not just to automatically accord one or other of them priority, but to consider in some cross-cultural perspective some of the ways they work together.

This is a more complex question than it may seem at first sight. It is easy to assume that there is just one right way for words, music and performance to be interrelated, and, correspondingly, just one self-evident method for conceptualizing it. But in fact there are untold diversities – and multiple controversies too. I have chosen my title as a way of leading into some of these debates, and at the same time of pointing to certain questions which, I suggest, need to be addressed for a full understanding.

We might start by reminding ourselves of a few of the many established approaches to analysing and interpreting song. Each carries its own implicit assumptions about what are the crucial dimensions in song – and thus which element in that sense comes first.

Still very much with us is the romantic view of song as the seat of primal creativity, of the natural unimpeded outpouring of human expression. That view has been eloquently expressed in a succession of evocative formulations over the centuries. As the eighteenth-century writer Anselm Bayly had it, 'that musick is the daughter of nature, appears from the aptitude, which children of all nations have, to singing freely as birds in the wood' (Bayly 1789: 2), while Wordsworth's poetry romantically pictures how the:

> *Feeding babe, didst in thy joy*
> *Sing at thy Mother's breast*
> (Wordsworth, *Michael*, 348–9).

The union of music and voice recall the lost Eden of natural innocence, just as Milton's invocation of the 'Blest pair of Sirens ... Voice and Verse' captures the evocative theme of the original primal song:

Sphere-born harmonious Sisters,
Voice and Verse
Wed your divine sounds, and mixt power employ ...

and bewails the loss of that first harmony, the 'state of good' (John Milton, *At a solemn music*). A similar romanticism has also at times shaped approaches to 'indigenous' and 'primitive' song. Thus 'oral poetry' (near synonym of 'song') has in the past been presented as the untouched vocalizations of people steeped in some primeval 'oral culture' before the literacy-bearing intrusion of colonialism.

These images of paradise and 'children of nature' still live on. But there has obviously been a marked reaction against them. Nowadays song (like oral poetry) is more often taken as culturally rather than 'naturally' formed – rooted in our fundamental human propensities certainly but, like language, varying in its cultural specificities. Within this broad approach, however, there is room for many different types of analysis.

There has in particular been a long and continuing scholarly tradition relating to the verbal element of songs. The varying perspectives that have risen and fallen within literary, linguistic and sociological theory were brought to bear on the texts, treated as verbal entities and documented in thousands upon thousands of written pages. The main focus was on genres that were – or were presumed to be – formulated or transmitted in writing; in the past it was only too often assumed that there could be little, if any, literary interest in forms that could be classified as *unwritten* or 'traditional'. But by now analyses of song lyrics, oral poetry and 'oral literature' generally are well established and interact with the multivariegated approaches to more 'conventional' written literatures.[1] Here the verbal texts have priority.

From the other end, the tools of established musicology have been engaged to analyse songs, primarily conceptualizing them as musical works encapsulated in notated scores. So-called 'popular' music has proved more resistant to this approach, not least because of the parallel assumption that, unlike notated works, it contained no real 'music' deserving of that name, certainly not worth serious musicological analysis. More recently, however, there has been greater elucidation of the *musical* patterns in popular songs and other performances, thus to an extent bridging the gap with traditional musicological analyses and drawing in a wider range of musicological approaches and debates (e.g. Berger 1999, Frith 2004a, 2004b, Menezes Bastos 1999, Walser 1993).

'Song' can also be seen as the combination of 'music' and 'poetry' (or 'literature'). Since these have commonly been envisaged as two distinct

---

1 For examples of this by now extensive work see Brown 1999, Finnegan 1992, Foley 2002, 2003, Okpewho 1992, 2004.

arts, there have in the past been various analyses comparing and/or contrasting them in general terms (e.g. Brown 1948, Burrows 1990, Kramer 1984, Winn 1981). These have noted, for example, the apparently shared features of music and poetry: their temporal and sequential qualities, and their deployment of rhythm and intonation. On the other hand, there is (arguably) the representational and cognitive nature of the verbal elements – able to describe and report on specifics in a way not open to music – contrasted to music with its eminent capacity for emotional and atmospheric expression. The model has often been of 'sense' as belonging to words, 'sound' and emotion to music.

Then there have been the many comments on the ways these apparently distinct arts of words and music can be tied together. These have often centred on the 'settings' of songs ('setting' words to music, that is), especially how words have been modified to fit a musical frame. The focus is often on a particular selection of Western art song with little consideration, for example, of issues raised by tonal languages (one interesting exception is the discussion of Vietnamese cases in Tran Quang Hai [2008]). But many illuminating points have been raised in the literature about how words and music work together and mutually affect each other in specific vocal genres – something I will return to.

There have been many approaches therefore to the relation of words and music. One further approach, however, merits particular attention and represents this chapter's main point of departure. This is to look at song, and at oral poetry, not as text but as performance.

The reality of performance

In a way it should be obvious that to analyse *sung* words, *chanted* words, we must understand them as performed, staged through the voice – after all, *singing* is itself often taken as a marker of 'performance'. But for a number of reasons, looking at song as performance has often *not* seemed obvious at all, and this notion is still often sidelined.

One factor here is the privileged position of *language,* something that runs deep in the long Western tradition of scholarly discourse. Anything which could not be captured in words or, at the least, described and analysed in words seemed not truly part of the academic domain – and for that reason not a serious part of human creation. The technologies of writing and print endorsed the substantiality and durability of written words. It was the verbal texts that apparently gave the 'real thing'. Small wonder that the written or writable words have so often been central in the study of songs; it is these that can be pinned down for analysis and transmission.

So it is that when we are faced with any art in which words play a part at all, we so readily look to its *textual writable* qualities. This is so of our analyses of the great human products from the past: of Homeric epics, Greek dramas, mediaeval troubadour song, traditional ballads, early madrigals. Often we only *have* the words, after all – or anyway little solid evidence about detailed performances – and it is to the words that we are accustomed to address our interest. We have the technology to handle them, and a host of well-honed approaches and vocabularies for their analysis. Even for the oral presentations or vocal performances of today it is often the *words* of a song that tend to be seized on. These, it is implied, are what define it, the mode in which it exists. So whether it is songs from far away and long ago or the genres of the present, it is in their words, their verbal texts, that their solidity and their potential for interpretation have seemed to lie.

Let me give a small illustration from my own experience. When I first embarked on anthropological fieldwork in West Africa my initial supposition was that for serious scholars 'the text' was the thing. That had been my experience in classical studies (the subject of my first degree): it was in written texts that the vocal productions of the past had come down to us.

The same paradigm runs through philology, history, folklore, literary analysis, and much else. *Texts* were the reality. So when I started research on African oral forms, including on their performance, I took for granted that to study them properly I had to transfer them onto a written page; it was only in that processed textual form that they could become proper objects for analysis, translation, commentary and ultimately publication. And this was not just a matter of convenience – a handy way to tie them down so they could be studied in the traditional manner. It was also, I gradually realized, the presupposition that it was in these transcribed words that their true essence lay. 'Performance' features were seen as contingent, secondary to the words' abiding existence in the verbal text. 'Song texts', 'lyrics', oral 'literature' – it was the *words* to which scholars should pay attention.

The wonderful story-telling performances that I encountered during my field work helped to change my perspective. But like others, I still had to struggle against the idea that verbal text was the central reality. For behind this again lay the entrenched Western story in which language is the key attribute of humanity – an assumption that has also sometimes shaped Western colonizers' views of indigenous peoples, linking together the (attributed) lack of verbal language with their (perceived) not-quite fully human status (Cláudia Neiva de Matos illustrates this well in the case of Brazil [2004: 231]). It is language furthermore, above all in its written form, which is so often conceptualized as the vehicle for modernity, rationality and the value of the intellect. In this still strikingly prevalent ideology, written language (especially when alphabetically printed) stands for the highest achievement of humanity.

It is scarcely surprising therefore that written formulations have seemed the appropriate way to represent the reality of African praises, Indian love songs, children's games, popular vocals, Christian hymns ... what counts are the words, with other elements sidelined as of lesser solidity. When you look up 'song' in a library catalogue you are faced with endless lists of predominantly verbal texts. That is where the true reality has so often been taken to lie – certainly not in ephemeral, uncapturable, performance.

This must seem strange when in songs the presence of music is indisputable; surely this acknowledges their existence as performance? But even this has commonly been interpreted in the context of that recurrent strand in Western thought which sees the intellectual dimension of humanness as lying in language, contrasting with the non-verbal and supposedly more emotionally driven elements within human beings. In the constructed opposition between the higher and the more bodily sides of human nature, music has not infrequently been assigned to the lower end, at least in its performed experiential qualities manifestations – an opposition, furthermore, sometimes extended into that between the (rational) West and the (emotion-driven) others. Here language stood for intellect and rationality, as against musical performance for the sensory, uncontrolled, even dangerous side of human nature (especially of course in non-elite or non-Western music), so it was to the words that scholars often preferred to give attention.

Some music to an extent escaped these associations: the high art genres that were mediated in notated form. Their scripted, and in a sense permanent, formulation gave them a claim to recognition together with the potential for scholarly musicological analysis. The prior and definitive existence of musical 'works', whether vocal or instrumental, could be attested not through ephemeral performances but in the score: the literate notated form toward which, it was sometimes assumed, music had gradually and rightly been evolving as part of the modernization process of the West.

It is no secret that there has been a decided reaction against this whole set of assumptions. This has come from several directions. One has been the transdisciplinary moves over the last generation or so towards an interest in process, dialogue and action, and away from defining the objects of study in terms of products, structures or definitive works. Rather than 'art', we now talk more about art*ists* and how they *do* things, the resources and constraints they cope with or the contexts and worlds in which they operate. Rather than looking just to fixed literary or musical 'works', we explore how people in practice create or experience them, in varied and perhaps fragmented or 'imperfect' ways. On the same lines, rather than '*the* song' we ask how people sing, compose and listen to songs, and their actions and emotions as they do so.

Going along with this have been decisive challenges to the narrowness of once-established canons of high art, literature or music. The arts of once-colonized and marginalized peoples, transnational hybrid genres and so-called 'popular culture' have inescapably and rightly become part of the scenario. Traditional forms of analysis increasingly appear inadequate.

Our developing appreciation of the literary genres of Africa, for example, has meant querying older definitions that envisaged literature as residing only in written text. In Xhosa praise poetry, Yoruba urban groups, South African migrant songs, Jamaican 'dub poetry' or Somali 'miniature' lyrics, the art lies not so much – or certainly not only – in the thin unilinear reproduction on a written page as in the modulations and arts of the performing voice(s). Indeed some posit the 'voice' as the key symbol and fulfilment of the artistry of the great African diaspora (as in Edward Brathwaite's *History of the Voice* 1984, also Peek and Yankah 2004: xii).

And this is not, of course, peculiar only to African forms. Performance and the arts of the voice play a central role in verbal genres throughout the globe – and in some written as well as unwritten ones too. Even for the songs of the past, for which we might seem to have only the bare written texts, we now realize that we can and should try to explore questions about their performance, sometimes with more success than might have been expected at the outset. The same interest in performance can be found both in the reinvigorated field of comparative literature (e.g. Gerstle, Jones and Thomas 2005, Valdés and Kadir 2004) and in the long continuing but perhaps now more integrated tradition of the training and styles of the singing voice and its interaction with differing instrumentations and technologies (cf. Potter 1998, 2000, Sell 2005). We are reminded that the irreducible core lies not in what can be inscribed on paper but in the deployed art of the voice in performance.

On the same lines, both ethnomusicology and the study of popular music have notably been challenging the traditional musicological conceptualization of music as the 'work' or notated score (see for example Berger 1999, Cavicchi 1998, Clayton et al. 2003, Feld et al. 2004, Hesmondhalgh and Negus 2002, Johnson 2000 and the overview collection in Frith 2004b). The analysis of musical *practices* takes us beyond musical texts and widens what counts as music: a recognition that there are many *musics*, not just one high-art form. So there is now a greater interest in the ethnographic investigation of how music and words are in practice actualized in performance, not excluding the ubiquitous commercial songs of today. This in turn has expanded our understanding of the key significance of performance in music, whether or not it also happens to have been pinned down in written scoring.

And then there are the changing technologies of communication. The model of the written as the core reality has not gone away, but it has been supplemented by more multimodal channels. Radio, with its remarkable potential for capturing and transmitting the voice in performance, has already moulded the perceptions of generations, giving solidity to the *sounds* of vocal music both alone and instrumentally surrounded. Multiple audio devices for both recording and listening have made song performances accessible to millions worldwide without the intervention of written texts, further amplified by multiple video and web options. Such technologies have directed our attention to new facets, helping us to capture and analyse how songs are *performed* – their actualized and fully rounded existence.

The upshot has been that looking to the substance of *performance* has become an increasingly recognized approach to analysing human creativity, especially (though perhaps not exclusively) those arts which, like the musical and verbal, are realized in temporal and sequential form.

This means that what the Finnish scholar Lauri Honko has dubbed '"The performance is king" paradigm' (Honko 2000: 13) has become one well-recognized framework for approaching vocally enunciated arts. The focus is on the embodied temporal substance of performance: its process, dynamics, experience, multimodal presence. 'Oral literature exists only in the here and now', is one way of putting it (Furniss 2004: 47), or 'There is no verbal art outside of performance' (Cancel 2004: 315). Here the primary form, the original, is the performance: *that* is what comes first.

Within performance

In this perspective, then, a song – or an oral poem – has its true existence not in some enduring text but in being *performed*: realized in a particular place and time through its activation of music, words, singing, perhaps too of somatic involvement, dance, colour, material display, brought together by co-creating agents in one immediate event. A song that in terms of its notated lyrics or melody might seem to be the 'same' item may be realized in very different ways in different renditions. The sung performance is evanescent, experiential, actualized, emergent in the participants' creation of the moment. As Peggy Phelan put it, 'performance's only life is in the present' (Phelan 1993: 146).

Here the voice is more than just a conduit for the transfer of already existing textualities, whether verbal or musical. The voice is *itself* part of the substance in its melodious, rhythmic, modulated presence. For a song's 'words' in a sense have no existence unless and until they are uttered, sung, brought forth with the due intonations, rhythms, timbres, pauses; nor has its 'music' until this is sounded by the voice. Here song and oral poetry mean the embodied activation of the human voice: speaking, singing, intoning, soloist, chorused, harmonizing, a cappella, instrumentally intertwined, amplified, distorted, mutually affected by differing forms of instrumentation, live, recorded – a whole host of varie-gated soundings for the human ear. In considering sung words we need to be attentive to the performers' vocal enactments, whether the microphone whispers of some modern singers, the distortions elaborated so effectively in certain styles, the 'pure' sounds of English cathedral choirs – and much much more.

To analyse a song as performance sidesteps questions about what comes, or should come, first. From this perspective the song's existence does not reside in either written literary text, musical work, or notated score, nor in some primal origin in human history or human nature. It is realized in the specificities of its performed actualization. In the enchanted moment of performance *all* the elements come together in a unique and perhaps ineffable experience, transcending the separation of its individual threads. And in that moment words, music and perhaps much else are *all* simultaneously prior, overlapping facets of a performed act that cannot be split apart.

Against that background there is a sense, then, in which it is irrelevant to ask about whether 'words' or 'music' come first. It is their integrated *performance* that is prior. But without undermining that very reasonable position, I would like to unpick the strands just a little. For it may prove illuminating to look more closely at the elements that are thus brought together in the realization of performance.

One set of questions that have often been explored is how the specific verbal and musical elements of a song have originated. It can be interesting to ask which in *that* sense comes first. This is at least in part an empirical and historically evidenced question. It is easy to start with the implicit expectation that there is one single route. It turns out – unsurprisingly, once we think about it – that there are diverse paths to composition.

Sometimes words and music are, at least in some sense, created together. But this 'togetherness' too has its variations. It can be *during* the performance itself – 'composition-in-performance' as it is sometimes described. This is one well-known pattern, exemplified in many lengthy sung narratives (South Slavic heroic songs are the classic case [Lord 1960]) or in the improvisations in song duels (e.g. Travassos 2000). Here in at least some senses the 'performance' could be said to come first. For neither that specific text nor its precise musical enactment had a separate autonomous existence prior to performance. Other cases of joint composition of the words alongside the music take place *before* the performed event – more, or less, that is, for this is scarcely a simple once-and-for-all matter (in some rock songs, for example, the lyrics may come relatively late in the lengthy process of partly joint prior composition) and there are varying degrees of stability in subsequent performances. The point, however, is that in such cases neither words nor music are created as independent self-standing entities.

But there are also many examples of just one element being created first, and separately. Sometimes it is the words. There are plentiful examples of words being composed by one author, either with the intention of their eventually appearing in musical form or (perhaps more often?) as a self-standing verbal piece, and this then being later – sometimes much later – set to music. This is quite often by someone else: 'text-setting' as it is often described. Sometimes several alternative musical versions have been created for the same words, by different composers. In other cases it is the music that is composed first with words created subsequently; 'Feito de oração' is one famous Brazilian example, where the lyrics were written by Noel Rosa specifically to fit Vadico's original piano composition (Menezes Bastos 1999). The same tune can be the base for totally differing lyrics or for words translated into differing languages (hymns are a good example of this). In some contexts – for example among urban musical groups in Fiji in the 1970s – creating a 'new song' often meant composing local words to an existing tune; similarly José de Moraes (2008) describes how the urban lyrics in São Paulo in 1920–1930s Brazil involved newly composed words set to already well-known tunes.

Arising from such examples of the separated composition of words and of music there has been extensive discussion of the relations between the 'music' on the one hand and the 'poetry' (or 'literature' or 'words') on the other (for example Ivey 1970, King 2001, Kramer 1984; also for earlier periods Harrán 1986, the perceptive historical perspective in Treitler 2003, and, for a modern example, Menezes Bastos 1999). Such discussion seems to be particularly prolific for the Western art song where these two elements have indeed often been identified as separate, and envisages the interaction between the ostensibly counter-strands of music and poetry as (variously) a matter of assimilation, of antagonism, of compromise, of re-creation. Various factors may be in play in these correlations. Meter, rhythm, melody, phrasing, repetition, stress, the commensurate or disparate alignment of syllables and notes, settings that are syllabic (one note per syllable) as against melismatic (many notes per syllable), multiple and overlapping as against single voices, the problems of stanzaic structures, the admixture (or not) of instrumental sounds, counterpoint, harmony – all these and more have been put under the microscope. So too have the emphases and emotions sometimes claimed for musically set as compared to spoken renditions.

All this obviously helps us to look into the intricacies of how music and words can work together. We also have to balance this, however, by recalling that whatever the compositional *origins*, a song's substance – its actualization – is also bound up with how these elements are in practice enacted and experienced in the temporal moment of performance.

There is also an issue about this juxtaposition between words and music. In certain circumstances it does indeed make good sense and applies well to some song-composition processes and in certain cultural contexts. In recent centuries of Western philosophy one common presupposition has indeed been the distinctiveness of language as against music. Their independent reality has also seemed assured by the practice of recognizing two distinctive and contrasting forms of enscription: alphabetic writing and notated score. But in the context of *performance* is this opposition always so evident? Are we justified in taking this distinction as something that can be universalized?

It has in fact been argued for some time that the juxtaposition of language versus music (or alternatively of speech versus song) should better be represented as, at best, a continuum rather than dichotomy (notably List 1963; also more recent discussions e.g. Banti and Giannatasio 2004, Herndon 1989, Feld and Fox 1994: 30–2, 35ff.). The classifications of different cultures vary after all and are differently conceptualized. Not all have a differentiated concept of 'music' and the genres of vocal expression can be divided up and defined in diverse ways: Koranic chanting may sound like a form of 'music' to outsiders, for example, but would not be so labelled by believers, while the classifications of Vietnamese 'spoken' as against 'sung' words described by Tran Quang Hai (2008) might seem surprising to uninformed Western ears. Such distinctions have no universal status but draw on a diversity of culturally differentiated features related to (among other things) intonation, melody, rhythm, styles of delivery, value systems and differing conceptual frameworks. There are multiple forms of vocal presentation ranging across a spectrum covering intoning, recitative, chanting, melodic singing, instrumental settings and much else. Any clear-cut line between all these based on some global opposition between language and music is likely to turn out both ethnocentric and impracticable.

Even in Western experience 'music' had a different coverage from now. Witness the Greek *mousiké* or medieval *musica* which just meant something *sung with words* (*cantus*), and where, as John Stevens put it, 'vocal music is found both in song (sung poetry) and in speech' (1986: 378). What we now know as punctuation marks were earlier the prompts for the speaker's or singer's delivery (phrasing and pauses for example), and it was on the model of such marks that the neumes or musical indications are thought to have developed – not a notation system to capture some separate entity called 'music', but cues to help singers' melodic delivery (Treitler 1984). And as Treitler comments, 'all the indications are that [the musicians in medieval song] would probably not have started out with an idea of words and music as separate expressive media that one could choose to unify or not' (Treitler 2003: 47, also 436ff.). Our contemporary dichotomy between 'words' and 'music' is not part of some abiding natural order.

In any case, neither 'language' nor 'music' are unitary concepts or unambiguous things-in-the-world. Each spans a plethora of both differing and overlapping properties, not all of which may be equally developed – or even present at all – in any given example. Any contrived opposition between them will inevitably be tendentious, at best selective, drawing on only certain of the elements that might be involved. The currently conventional juxtaposition of language and music often invokes a rather artificial opposition between the performed arts of music on the one hand and the supposedly 'plain' language of so-called 'everyday speech' on the other. But linguists are now stressing the performed (rather than purely referential) dimensions of *all* vocal expression, and the creative and acoustic poetics with which we speak. The music/language contrast no longer looks so self-evident. We might do well in any case to query the model of some generalized 'everyday speech' and/or 'plain' written prose as the 'natural' or 'unmarked' form which comes first and is then somehow built on and changed for more sophisticated or decorated expression. Rather, all cultures recognize a variety of 'speech genres' (as Bakhtin [1986] famously has it) – what I might perhaps prefer to call 'vocalized genres' to cover the full range here – each with their own poetics which are likely to include, among other things, their expected sonic, rhythmic, prosodic, timbral and other performance features.

Thus even in genres that in traditional English circles might be labelled as 'poetry' rather than 'song', performers draw on the acoustic and intonational arts of the voice, on non-verbal as well as linguistic resources, emotion as well as cognition. When I hear, for example, recordings of T. S. Eliot declaiming his poetry or Edith Sitwell performing *Façade* or, indeed, a reading of one of Shakespeare's sonnets, the sense has some meaning for me but the *sound* patternings also come through as crucial. Sound and the artistry of the voice are surely essential in *all* genres of performed verbal art (is this not part of what we mean by 'poetry'?). Across the world performed poetry depends for its realization on (among other things) the performer's exploitation of sound. From the raucous and vehement tones of a Xhosa praise poet, magical Kuna chants or Jewish liturgical cantillation to the emotion-laden dirges of Caucasian Georgian women, Shokleng ritual wailing, or the Kaluli lamentations that Steven Feld well describes as 'melodic-texted-sung weeping' (Opland 1998, Sherzer 1990, Banti and Giannatasio 2004: 305, Kottthoff 2001, Urban 1988, Feld 1995), or, no less, the latest local dance song – all these resonate through the sounding voice.

To try to match all these and more onto some neat division between music and words is to miss their multiplicity and range. It might be more helpful to think not of music versus language but of the complex modes of human vocal artistries. Thus poetry and song can be seen as shorthand terms for the spectrum of ways that people deploy sonic properties in their vocal presentations – musicalize them, one might say, in diverse and relative ways across a series of overlapping and varying dimensions such as intonation, rhythm, timbre, onomatopoeia and much else, sometimes in conjunction with instrumental sounds and multisensory expression. It is sometimes convenient – and in some cultures acceptable – to focus down on aspects of these multifarious and diversely deployed dimensions under the solid-sounding concepts of 'words' and 'music'. But these terms need to be understood as if in quotation marks. It is in that light that I will continue to use them here, mindful that we are dealing not with separate things but with certain relative, elusive, selective and inevitably multiplex dimensions of the ways humans deploy the arts of the voice.

For the central point here is that songs are made possible through the multiple ways in which that flexible and remarkable instrument, the expressive human voice, draws on and exploits a vast and complex set of auditory resources. Some of these are to an extent signalled within written texts – rhyme, alliteration, assonance, rhythm, repetition, parallelism, pauses, structural organization such as line and verse – but these are only a small sample. Others are less apparent in writing but are captured well by the human ear, to some extent assisted by modern audio technologies, like the subtleties of volume, pitch, tempo, intonation, texture, intensity, emphasis, timbre, onomatopoeia, silence – an astounding range of variegated resources. And then there are all those near-infinite modes of delivery: spoken, sung, recited, intoned, musically accompanied or mediated, shouted, whispered, sighed, wept, amplified, carried by single or multiple or alternating voices. Once again we need to bear in mind the complex spectrum of *all* the resources marshalled by vocal performers rather than some simplified allocation between words versus music.

Let me now turn to a further series of questions about what goes on within the enactment of performance. I have been speaking so far as if the voice and its 'words' form an essential core in the performance as a whole. In focusing on 'sung words' we have naturally been taking the voice's enunciation as central to our concerns.

But is this too an over-simplification? We can all probably recall examples where one or another element of a performance has drawn our particular attention. So it might be productive to ask which particular dimensions are pre-eminent in a particular performance of sung words so as to unwrap some of its many intertwined strands. As people perform and listen, what for *them* 'comes first'?

The obvious and perhaps unthinking answer might self-evidently seem to be 'the words'. That at least is what the scholarly analyst, hooked on text, is likely to conclude for any performance in which words play any part at all (and I am aware that this is the element with which my own work has been primarily concerned). Focusing on the words – insofar as they can be separated out – will continue to be illuminating; there is no reason to confine such analyses just to the traditional canon of written literature. But does it follow that they are therefore necessarily the most important element in the song as actualized in performance? How far they are – or are not – is again an empirical question to be explored ethnographically rather than in the abstract. And the answers are diverse: they vary for different genres, historical contexts, even individuals.

It is a complicated question, for there are several senses in which 'the words' might – or might not – take a leading role. One thing is the degree of textedness. The concept of 'textuality' is an elusive and debated one, especially in the context of performed verbal art; I will not try to pursue this here, except to say that it is a relative rather than absolute matter and the textuality of songs varies (in this respect as in some others, 'song' itself has to be a relative notion). But it is unquestionable that sometimes the sung vocalizations amount to little that could be transferred readily, if at all, into recognizable written words. The words may have little coherence or substance, may even be minimal in the extreme (that is not to say that they may not be extremely effective in performance: the few words may be repeated many times over and/or work together with the music to create an intensity of praise, mourning, celebration, and so on). As against this, other songs have highly organized, elaborated and/or lengthy verbalized textual substance – eminently reproducible in writing.

Another strategy might be to look to the cognitive meaning, the dimension of language especially emphasized in Enlightenment-shaped conceptualizations. From that perspective it is clear that the relative significance of 'sense' to 'sound' (if I may put it that way) varies in vocal utterances, whether or *not* musically set. Sometimes the cognitive, propositional meaning is indeed strong. But there are also many examples of poetry (spoken as well as sung) where the meaning seems elusive indeed but where the sonic experience and auditory beauty carry us along – or indeed one could say that it is *that* which communicates meaning rather than, or as much as, the words (I am doubtful about analyses which picture the 'words' as carrying 'meaning', music 'merely' 'emotion'). This certainly sometimes happens in song where the propositional meaning of the words can take second place. Simon Frith points out well how singers in popular music communicate not just by verbal devices but through:

> emphases, sighs, hesitations, changes of tone; lyrics involve pleas, sneers and commands as well as statements and messages and stories (which is why singers like the Beatles and Bob Dylan in Europe in the 1960s would have profound significance for listeners who didn't understand a word they were singing). (Frith 2004a: 203)

Sometimes the words are *expected* not to be intelligible in a cognitive sense, or anyway not to all participants. They may be meant for some restricted in-group alone or addressed to 'God' rather than human listeners (a point well made by Potter [1998: 32] of medieval polyphony). They may be in a foreign or exclusive language, or just not very significant in the performance as a whole. During my own fieldwork I was somewhat ashamed of my failure to record many song texts. I later came to recognize that in many of these Limba songs, particularly those performed by acclaimed experts, the words were by most people regarded as esoteric and, as far as I could see, not especially attended to. For most participants the prime focus seemed to be the sung, instrumental and partly chorused music, the embodied, rhythmic and circularly spaced dynamic of dance, and perhaps the visual glamour of costume. We know in any case that many familiar songs contain words that are nonsensical in strict referential terms: all those 'fal la la's, 'badap's and 'yeh yeh yeh's, or lines constantly ending with 'o', 'a', 'e-ye' and so on. In many genres it can be the sonic effectiveness of the performance together with the broad expectations created through listeners' knowledge of the relevant conventions and repertoire that shapes the experience rather than the cognitive verbal content.

There is also another sense in which 'words' may or may not come 'first': the place of the vocal line itself within the whole. This is in part a practical matter of the overall musical structure – the words generally being more prominent in monophonic as against polyphonic music, for example. Also, other things being equal, words usually come through more clearly from a vocal line carried by a single voice than from several, especially of course where voices overlap, sing the same words at different times or on top of each other, and so on. Words by chorus singers are often harder to hear and identify than those by solo voices. Various devices can help, like repetitions, refrains, alternations between solo and chorus lines, prior knowledge, or, in some traditions, programme notes – all part of the context for the relative projection or submergence of the verbal element within the performance as a whole. And then of course the vocal line(s) may be only part of, even subservient to, instrumental lines in the midst of which the vocalized words may have a relatively minor role.

Amid all these complexities it is indeed hard to sort out just what the role of 'words' is (even where we are clear just what we mean by 'words' here). But rather than generalized conclusions, we do need to regard this as an open question that needs investigating for particular cases. In some oral performances the words *do* indeed seem in some sense to have pride of place – in Somali classical poetry, for example, or the epic narratives of South Slavic heroic singers or of West African tellers narrating the deeds of the legendary Sunjata. The same might be said of, for example, Yoruba praise poetry, Gregorian chant, recitative in opera or oratorio, declaimed myths, chanting of the Koran, intoned sermons and speeches. Here the words indeed seem to play a key role: in this sense they do come first.

But then there are other cases. In Shona *mbira* music in Central Africa the poetic song texts accompany the instrument rather than the other way round (according to Berliner 1976), just as for women singers in late twentieth-century Zimbabwe it was 'not the script of the songs that mattered most but rather the sound coming over radio waves, on a cassette, or live, and staying in people's memories and their consciousness' (Gunner 1994: 2). David Coplan comments on the songs of Basotho migrants in South Africa:

To a Western observer like myself, the melodic declamation of literally hundreds of lines in a sefela [Basotho migrants' song] performance made these songs appear powerfully text-driven. Yet in discussions and inter-views, performers repeatedly advised me to focus on rhythm and melody as keys to the understanding of compositional creativity. As the singer-poet Makeka Likhojane – in Sesotho one of the likheleke, 'eloquent ones' – explained firmly in deflecting the exegesis of an opaque metaphorical passage: 'If you want to understand my song, mister, just listen to the music.' (Coplan 1994: 9)

In much popular music today, as Simon Frith points out, good song lyrics 'score' the performance not 'in the words themselves ... [but] by the music' (Frith 1996: 181). The words of songs may be easily forgotten, even by the singers themselves, while the music is remembered (for an example see Menezes Bastos 1999). Ethnographic studies of popular music have stressed that, as Robert Walser puts it of heavy metal, 'Verbal meanings are only a fraction of whatever it is that makes musicians and fans respond to and care about popular music' (1993: 26). For any specific example of song the relative significance of the words may not be easy to assess definitively – but if we want to understand the full reality we need to explore the question.

It is partly a matter of whose viewpoint you take, for even for the same genre of song there may be plural assessments. For the composer or lead vocalist the words may indeed feel central – but are they equally so for all the performers in a group? For a back-line chorus member, drummer, bass, second violinist, accompanist ...? There may be differences in outlook and experience, even perhaps internal struggles about which musical line predominates, and which wins out at different points as the performance unfolds. Or again, I think of Simon Ottenberg's comments on the moving performances of the blind Limba musician, Sayo, who composes and performs songs pervaded by a sense of sadness and misfortune. But these sorrowful songs 'do not create evident sorrow for the chorus' for *they* are less concerned with the words than with the enjoyment of responding in song, clapping, dancing (Ottenberg 1996: 92–3). And even for choral singers in complex instrumental or fugal ensembles – in classical oratorio, for example – the words may fade into the background as against the complexities of the intertwining musical lines. Sometimes the words are experienced as a kind of meaningless fill-in to keep the music going, especially if they are in a foreign or esoteric language. Does every chorus member think about the literal meaning of *Kyrie eleison* as they follow out the complex musical lines, or take seriously all the words being projected through their voices?

It is also worth considering the *listeners'* experience – the practice, not just the ideal. If we are honest, we have to recognize that we sometimes just do not hear the words! This does of course to some extent relate to the particular genre, texture and delivery. But how many of us have on occasion been unable, as listeners, to make out all the words being sung? What is more, even if we deplore this in theory, we tend to accept it provided other dimensions are effective. Is the verbal element in practice sometimes more marginal than we think?

Once again we need to be warned against too ready generalization, for even individuals may vary, and for the same performance. Springsteen fans, for example, may 'listen to' different aspects in a performance:

> I am the one [says the wife] ... that concentrates on the music and Chris [my husband] hears the lyrics ... I love these songs ... but I can't sit down

and write (or even sing along, for that matter) all of the lyrics. Chris on the other hand ... knows the lyrics of every song he's ever heard. (Cavicchi 1998: 111)

It remains a question to be investigated in practice rather than assumed in advance as to how important the vocalized words of a song are, for whom, and in what sense. Recordings raise the same questions as live performances. Here again there is more diversity to explore than the easy generalizations – or indeed, our sometimes idealized conceptualizations – would suggest.

We also need to remind ourselves that performed songs may not be just *acoustic* events but also, like much human communication (see Finnegan 2002), draw simultaneously on a range of multimodal resources. Active performance, both live and even to some extent recorded, is not just audition. It is worth again recalling Isidore Okpewho's wise reminder that in oral performance: 'the words spoken are only part of a general spectacle designed to please both the ears and the eyes' (Okpewho 1992: 48). The visual, the somatic, gestural, theatrical, material – all may enter in. So too may movement, whether or not heightened as dance, and the interaction of many bodies and presences. It is not just words – or even just music and words – but multisensory enactment. The role of the 'words' can only really be assessed in this wider, multidimensional perspective – sometimes to the fore but sometimes perhaps taking a more submerged role in relation to the other components of performance. Each case has really to be considered on its merits rather than by prior presupposition.

All this is not to denigrate the significance – the wonder – of the verbal textualities. Rather it is to recognize their polyfunctional and multiform diversities and the importance of their performed settings. For if we are to take sung *words* seriously, we must do more than just take their presence for granted. We must also recognize their diverse styles, the varying guises in which they appear and the differing roles they may have in performance, sometimes to the fore, sometimes in more elusive and muted, but still complex, ways, and – as with any form of vocal poetics – deployed in the context of specific genre expectations which may or may not attach particular priority to their referential meaning or coherence.

Beyond performance?

Let me return again to the reality of performance. Recognizing this has been salutary indeed. It has rightly challenged certain ethnocentric Western assumptions and elitist restrictions, and revealed dimensions which the focus on written text and on limited high art genres had in the past dismissed as of little significance. We can approach 'words' and 'music' not by considering their abstract relationships or by their printouts on the written or notated page, but in how they are actualized in the integrated circumstances of a performance.

But has this sometimes gone too far? Can we wholly accept the view that sung words are only in the here-and-now or have no real existence outside of performance? Is it reasonable to hold that ultimately it is *only* in performance that the chanted word has its true existence and fulfilment? That first and foremost always comes performance?

There are also senses in which sung words do *not* after all exist solely in the vanishing performance moment. In one way, of course, every performance is unique and with its own features: its mix of communicative channels; its particular place and timing; its participants with their own perspectives; the detailed performance arrangements, music, singing, movement – all the elements that enter into one given event in the passing temporal moment. But at the same time it does not stand on its own or appear out of nothing. To quote Lauri Honko again:

> Any performance is a compromise, an intelligent adaptation of tradition within unique situations structured by a confluence of several factors. It can be understood only against a broader spectrum of performances of the same integer in similar and different contexts. (Honko 2000: 13)

In other words, a performance, however original, is shaped in relation to known stylistic and contextual expectations. Even if disrupting them, it draws on them. Memories of other enactments colour the occasion. 'Performance, even in its dazzling physical immediacy, drifts between present and past, presence and absence, consciousness and memory', Elin Diamond writes, and 'embeds features of previous performances' (1996: 1).

What participants bring with them to a performance shapes its meaning. Performance is not just a single event, a situated burst of sound and movement, living only 'in the present'. It may indeed be created in the magic experiential moment – but *also* rooted in or reverberating with something more abstracted, detachable from the flow, imbued with memories and connotations for its participants which go *beyond* the immediate moment.

So the focus on performance is now being balanced by a revival of interest in 'text' and 'textuality' – or at any rate in the 'something' (it will not necessarily be verbal) by virtue of which any performance is itself more than just the performing moment (see for example Barber 2003). On a specific occasion the words may be blurred, perhaps, the acoustics unsatisfactory, even some potential elements missing, poorly executed or (by some standards) over-elaborated. But because listeners and performers have encountered the song on other occasions or have read it in textual form, sung it themselves, know it in audio or video form, or, at the least, are acquainted with the general characteristics of the genre, they can recognize a musically and verbally characterized performance as a familiar and graspable one. To understand performed songs we need to look to their participants' experiences and knowledge beyond as well as within the performances.

And that brings us to the common human experience of transformation among and between media. We all in practice work with many media. It is nowadays commonplace to criticise the translation of dynamic performance into cold print; and in one sense this is indeed an unforgivable mangling of the vibrancy of performance – one reason why the subtleties of African oral poetry or urban popular music were so long unappreciated by outsiders reliant on written transcripts. But in practice such transfers between media are constantly happening, and in a variety of directions. European (or notionally 'European') ballads, for example, have been realized through diverse media, both concurrently and sequentially – in writing, in print (broadsheets, pamphlets, and so on), in live sung or spoken performance, in pictures, in broadcast and in electronic modes; and travelled and been changed in various guises throughout the globe – and these recontextualizations recognized in at least some sense and some contexts as somehow versions of the same thing. Similar transformations are a common pattern across genres of Africa and the diaspora, just as Brazilian popular song and literature give many examples of not only live performances but also circulation in pamphlets etc. as well as in radio and recordings (e.g. Travassos 2000; also more generally dos Santos 2004).

In this sense too a performance may not, after all, be unique, for it is likely to carry memories and overtones of other modes and re-creations. A song can be experienced – can exist – in a live performance, on a printed page, an audio cassette, gramophone record, video, CD, radio or TV broadcast, downloaded from the web, discussed on email, transmitted on mobile phone; or it can be recited from memory, re-created aloud or 'in the head', in bits, or bringing out just some of its dimensions but not others. And all of these modes are viable forms of actualization as far as their human practitioners are concerned. The specific options vary through the ages, of course; the current emphasis on recording and electronic technologies is a particular feature of much contemporary song, for example. But the basic experience of reincarnations and interactions in multiple media – all this is not just a pursuit of academic researchers but a far from unusual part of human culture.

This is something we need to take account of even where our prime focus is actualized performance; it is not helpful to try to romanticize some 'authentic', 'original' context as the 'true' performance with other recontextualizations being somehow 'secondary' or 'artificial'. For any particular event some or all of the listeners may already have experience of the song – or something like it – as, for example, a written text, audio recording, live performance, television broadcast, video, film, webcast ... or other forms again. The words of Bruce Springsteen's songs are enacted as live musical events; but they are also re-experienced outside the performance situation and built into the fabric of the fans' lives – discussed with other fans, memorized from lyric sheets, recited to others, quoted in emails and letters (Cavicchi 1998: 110ff). For some performed genres there may be only a limited number of such interchanges. For others there are extensive traditions of exegesis and of acquaintance with variously mediated forms, all of which provide the interpretations with which people both come to a performance and in turn carry forward their understandings into other media.

That means that performances of sung words may be shot through with an experience of written forms (and not just in the so-called 'literate West' but in Africa and Asia and those 'other' cultures once somewhat exaggeratedly differentiated as 'oral' but in fact both now and for longer than often realized in close touch with writing). Other performances may be coloured by their video or electronic presentations.

Written versions, too, can be imbued with the echoes of performance. Once we have deeply experienced the sung rendition of some particular song – in audio, video, live performance, through our own singing – can we ever read its verbal text without reimagining its performed version, without hearing and seeing something more than the printed lines? Earlier I quoted from Milton's 'Blest pair of Sirens ... Voice and Verse'. But I have also sung those same words in the choral version by the English composer Hubert Parry, and now find it impossible to read the words, either aloud or to myself, without the rhythms and melodies and harmonies and dynamics of its sung performance ringing dominantly through my ears and body. Menezes Bastos similarly mentions how João Cabral de Melo Neto could no longer see his *'Morte e vida S/severina'* as a poem after it had been turned into a song (1999: 82). Sung words have these varying layers of complexity: actualized in performance certainly, but often inextricably resonating with multimedia evocations *beyond* the single event.

So if performance in one sense lies at the heart of sung words, we *also* need to explore how far they are also situated in a life of mingled modalities. Perhaps none automatically comes first, for we move through their admixture and in a way carry all – to one degree or another – with us. The magic moment of performance, in one sense the crux of it all, does not in every sense come first or stand alone.

So ...

There are many ways then that we can look at the concatenation of words, music and performance that makes up song, and many senses in which we can ask which 'comes first' or how they interact; or indeed whether in some contexts it makes any sense at all to identify them as separate things or to ask about their priority. We can bring established literary and musicological approaches to bear in examining the verbal and musical texts; and that itself is already a vast array of insights – provided of course that we recognize that in doing so we are inevitably conceptualizing certain dimensions at the expense of others. There are many further complexities to explore if we look into performance and at the problematic interaction, balance and blurring between what we see as 'words' and 'music' and their diverse manifestations – diverse because there is no one 'right' or 'natural' way in which the human voice speaks and sings, no single way to conceptualize and classify its actions. We need to look beyond the single performance too, into the multivariegated experiences people bring with them of other performances and other mediations.

But amid all these complexities, a full appreciation must still surely include a recognition of the staged, performed actuality of sung words enacted by the voice. Here musicalized and verbalized dimensions – and much else too – come together, shaped in the action of that gathered performing moment.

And if we are right to be sceptical about the more extreme romanticist perspectives on song as 'natural' or 'primeval', with their ethnocentric and patronizing baggage, still we can accept that there is still something of enchantment – en-chantment – about words that are *sung*. There is a rich and marvellous range of complex possibilities. Throughout the globe the singing voice continues to bind those wonderful dimensions of human culture together – verbal, musical, performed – in the miraculous voicing of sung words.

7

Competence and performance:
Was Chomsky right after all?

Language is … ?

I have long been unsympathetic to the idea of 'competence' in linguistic expression, which I associate with Chomsky's highly dry and abstract approach, broadly (it seems) anti-performance, practice, emergence – key ideas in much recent sociolinguistic and anthropological writing.. But some recent personal experiences (described a little later) have led, to my surprise, to my seeing some value in the idea of language as having some kind of existence prior to its formulation in performance.[1]

When I visited Paris in 2009 for a debate generously hosted by Jean Derive and Ursula Baumgardt, I was concerned about my incompetence in French. But I then hit on an excellent set of audio recordings and phrase books. I was much struck by the opening chapter in one of them. The first and most important step, it said, was to learn the gestures and facial expressions of a different target language.

I'm not sure I succeeded. But I did warm to the idea of the priority of gesture. Or, at the least, of considering gesture as part of speech – something I was first taught by Limba co-creating audiences and story-tellers (cf. Finnegan 1967, 1970) and have argued for more explicitly in more recent works (cf. Finnegan 2003, 2007, 2011a, 2011b), and now part of one body of linguistic theory – something that perhaps we Africanists are especially alert to.

We know for example how, as the wonderful scholar Kwabena Nketia tells us, what seems for a moment static in the music may be relieved by the text or the dynamic quality of the movements that accompany it. Similarly, the appearance of a masked dancer in a performing arena may reinforce the essence and intention of the occasion and give added meaning to the musical and dance forms (cf. Nketia 1996: 126). Or again, I recall Kelly

---

1 Since a first attempt to tackle these issues was at a conference in Paris, this chapter has benefited from the international and, especially, the Parisian insights provided there.

Askew's study of popular bands and ensembles (2002) where 'performing the nation' in Tanzania relies on the music and dance, not just the song texts, while in the South African rap band Prophets of Da City the ruptured lyrics do indeed receive attention but at the same time have to be heard ('it is crucially rhythm, rhyme, verbal inflection, and the syncopation of these with sound and beat') and are articulated through 'music, dance, style, and the associated activities of hip-hop culture, including graffiti or spray-can art' (Brown 2003: 159, 145).

In radio, words jostle with music, cooperating and at times competing, and no doubt sometimes carrying differing priorities for differing listeners and situations. In film, long a familiar medium in Africa, spoken or sung verbal dimensions may be relatively prominent, in this sense comparable to other genres of verbal art; but language does not always lie at its heart, for crucial roles are taken by visual manifestations, by music and other sonic input, sometimes by dance – all of which make it possible, as with the popular indigenous films in Nigeria, to communicate polyvocally across linguistic boundaries (described in Okome 1995).

The web has further examples of multidimensional expression, coming in a host of different combinations, sometimes privileging the verbal (seldom exclusively), more often intershot with the visual and sonic dimensions that are now increasingly deployed by performers from both Africa and beyond (cf. Kaschula 2003) (see Finnegan 2007: 216 from which these examples are drawn). It does not apply just to Africa, of course. Increasingly evidence-based linguists are pointing to the significance of multisensory dimensions of language (see for example the 1994 *Encyclopedia of Language and Linguistics* conclusion that 'the central element of [language] is verbal but [it] contains as an essential component a substantial non-verbal element, e.g. intonation, stress, punctuation, etc.': Asher and Simpson 1994, vol. 10: 5137).

Adam Kendon in a powerful and convincing series of publications (not enough known) has well signalled the complementary roles of gesture and speech – an approach that might in principle be applied to other oral genres too:

> Participants in conversation ... use gesture and speech in partnership and can shift the respective roles of gesture and speech in the utterance from one moment to the next in ways that seem rhetorically appropriate ... The two modes of expression employ different media which have different possibilities ... Gesture can be useful as a way of exhibiting overarching units of meaning, as a way of keeping visible an aspect of meaning throughout the course of a spoken utterance or even after the speech has finished. Gesture and speech ... serve different but complementary roles. (Kendon 2000: 61)

Simon Frith similarly points out how good song lyrics 'score' the performance not 'in the words themselves ... [but] by the music' (Frith 1996: 181). All this is of course consistent with an approach I and others have long espoused. It is one, furthermore, that fits well into that syndrome of scholarship where cultural anthropology, folklore, literature, cultural studies and performance studies intersect.

Put more succinctly, this is founded in the pragmatist tradition that has so illuminatingly affected many disciplines, not least that approach to language that turns the spotlight not on formal features but on the uses of language in context. With foundations in the pragmatist bent of earlier scholars like John Dewey or Kenneth Burke, anthropologists like Franz Boas and Bronislaw Malinowski, and J. L. Austin's philosophical theory of speech acts and performative utterances, pragmatics is by now a recognized field within studies of language. Though not all scholars might align themselves with this terminology, a recent summary is right to draw attention to the intrinsically interdisciplinary perspective shaping this general stance, characterizing it as 'an approach to language which takes into account the full complexity of its cognitive, social and cultural (i.e. meaningful) functioning in the lives of human beings' (Verschueren 2009: 19).

This action- and context-oriented perspective on language is now evident across a range of areas, among them sociolinguistics, speech act theory, ethnomethodology, reception studies, conversation analysis, performance studies, linguistic anthropology and the ethnographies of communication. As exemplified vividly in M. M. Bakhtin's work – by now a major influence – it extends to both 'ordinary' and 'literary' language (Finnegan 2011a, b). Downplaying the significance of linguistic and grammatical technicalities or formalist and structuralist approaches to text, it has turned scholars' eyes rather toward process and context and, beyond this, to the role of multiple participants and voices in the actual practices of communication – something which demands study in specific cultural and historical realization rather than (as in much of Chomsky's work) in abstract, judgemental or universalizing terms.[2] It takes us beyond a limited canon of texts recognized by elite scholars into how people are actually acting – performing and entextualizing – in more popular forms and in the present of everyday living.

The pragmatist concern with words used in the context of action rather than with language as an abstract, primarily cognitive or independent system has shaped the account here. One thread in this general approach has been especially far-reaching. This is the unfolding perspective associated with linguistic anthropology – so called for short, but in practice a notably interdisciplinary set of endeavours extending across literary and theatre studies as well as sociolinguistics, folklore and art. Its basic assumption, well summarized by Alessandro Duranti, is that 'to understand the meaning of linguistic messages one must study them within the contexts in which they are produced and interpreted' (2009: 31). Duranti notes too the

---

2 For recent overviews, see Cummings 2010, Robinson 2006, Verschueren and Östman 2009; also background in Clark 1996, Harris 1998.

shift, evident since the 1960s, 'from an interest in what language encodes (reference, denotation) to what language does (performance)' (2009: 32; also 1997, 2004).

A signal move was the so-called 'breakthrough into performance' first enunciated in anthropology and folklore. By now this has pervaded many disciplines, a highly productive strand running across literary, cultural and sociolinguistic studies and also crystallizing in the now established field of performance studies (cf. Schechner 2006). It signalled a break with a prime focus on fixed text and challenged the once taken-for-granted model of literary works as self-contained decontextualized entities. Scholars working from this orientation have produced a series of illuminating insights into, for example, reflexive language, dialogism, intertextuality and genre. Let me highlight in particular the cross-cultural collection *Responsibility and Evidence in Oral Discourse* (Hill and Irvine 1993) and Richard Bauman's seminal *A World of Others' Words: Cross-Cultural Perspectives on Intertextuality* (2004) with its eye to intertextuality as communicative practice through an analysis of both oral performances and literary records.

Linguistic anthropology's comparative orientation has at the same time rightly challenged analyses with limited ethnocentric Western perspectives and forwarded insights from explicitly cross-cultural studies.[3] A further strand is a view of language as multilayered and dialogic. This de-empha-sizes concepts of structure and fixity, and envisages speaking and writing – and communicating more generally – as active process and exchange. Texts are multisided and multivoiced and the use of others' voices is nothing strange. Now undergoing a revival of interest from several direc-tions, Bakhtin's classic accounts (1973, 1981, 1986) have brought out how in both talk and literary text what we say or write is in one way or another suffused with others' voices. Sometimes, as he says, these are openly intro-duced and clearly demarcated (in quotation marks):

> Echoes of the change of speech subjects and their dialogical interrelations can be heard clearly here. But any utterance, when it is studied in greater depth ... reveals to us many half-concealed or completely concealed words of others with varying degrees of foreignness ... furrowed with distant and barely audible echoes. (Bakhtin 1986: 93)

On similar lines Erving Goffman too has well alerted us to the complex and multisided role of others' words in the enstaging of everyday life and the diverse forms of speech within it:

---

3 Notably in Bauman 1977, Ben-Amos and Goldstein 1975, Hymes 1975, 1977. Also Bauman 2004, Bauman and Briggs 1990, Duranti 2001, Duranti and Goodwin 1992, Hanks 1996, Hill and Irvine 1993, Hymes 1996, Mannheim and Tedlock 1995, Silverstein and Urban 1996, Urban 1991.

> Words we speak are often not our own, at least not our current 'own'
> ... We can as handily quote another (directly or indirectly) as we can say
> something in our own name. ... Deeply incorporated into the nature of talk
> are the fundamental requirements of theatricality. (Goffman 1981: 3, 4)

In such perspectives the significance of context, of multiple voices and of language as action, the perspectives going under the label of 'postmodernism' have played a part, interacting with other ongoing studies and debates. To this syndrome of approaches let me bring a new perspective, and, if you will allow me, a very personal approach.

I happened to mention to my daughter – a sports fan or, rather, the mother of highly successful sports sons – that I was attending a conference on competence and performance. She was puzzled that I should be involved in something so relevant and up-to-date. She explained what she meant: that to her these terms meant something very different from that in linguistics. In the growing and increasingly serious subject of sports psychology, competence might indeed be the necessary condition, but without training – and protracted, long-focused training – competence was never sufficient. The same was true of other skills – and arts – such as music or chess, where the dominant metaphor had long been one of 'innate talent' or of the special almost supra-human 'genius' of individuals like Mozart and Judit Polgar. Only after years of specialized training, it emerged from psychological research, could such skills flourish (summed up in the popular but excellently written and referenced *Bounce* by Matthew Syed [2011]).

Not only this wider literature but my own experiences too have made me more sensitive to something that I suppose I knew – or should have done – already but, like many others whose work I admire, had chosen to ignore for the focus on performance. That is, that language is not after all the same as speech.

Speech is, indeed, creative performance. How could it be otherwise? And how could anyone who knows about speaking be cajoled by Noam Chomsky's irrational, or at best unfounded, speculative abstractions? Speech is not primarily cognitive but, as I discovered time after time in my own illness, something with a physical base. The reason for this is personal example – true to my qualitative base, I am not above using a single 'anecdotal' case study to convey my meaning. I recently spent two weeks in hospital. The reason was that, though unaware of it myself, my friends and family had become increasingly convinced that I was suffering from the first stages of dementia and had arranged for me to be taken to hospital by emergency ambulance.

It was during that time in hospital that (with one marginal exception in a departmental seminar a couple of weeks earlier) I first noticed my main – and, to me, only – symptom: an inability to give voice to words which I had clearly in my mind and longed to utter, together with some spasms in my right hand – all this much more pronounced and more noticeable to others.

In my recollection this was always when I was longing to say something to someone close to me – daughter or husband, but also at least once on the telephone to my sister. The obstruction seemed to go on for hours – in practice maybe only half a minute – and was utterly frustrating, even more so I imagine for the hearer than for me (it was always something I really, really wanted to say, but not I think of any particularly deep or buried meaning). Following that fit, as it were, I then seemed to return to normal and was perfectly able to speak if started on a new subject.

This reminded me that I had always believed my New Zealand researcher friend, a neurologist, that the basis of speech is physical (which I gather is a controversial view among psychologists) and for the first time thoroughly understood from the inside what that meant. I was thinking perfectly clearly, even (I think) in intended words, but could not physically bring them through my lips.

This fitted furthermore with my conviction that speech and performance are intimately interwoven. It has also since made me more consciously aware of the creativity of language use, both spoken and written. Before either, I now see that I hesitate between a number of possible terms – something I do not believe is allowed for in Chomsky's more prescriptive analyses. Some are more or less synonymous (no words completely are perhaps), some have different shades of meaning or connotation. My final choice might in each case have been otherwise, and to compensate for this I often in speech (and sometimes in writing) go on to use several of them, piling up terms in a way that might seem – but is not (I now realize) – redundant.

I have found the whole experience fascinating in intellectual as well as personal terms. It has been amplified and in a sense clarified by my parallel experience of dreams – potentially but not yet actualized verbal stories and poems ready in my mind to be dictated writing. The potential words came – and come: words in that mysterious boundary between dreaming and waking, an area which, I am coming to think, is fundamental to our consciousness but almost totally unknown to our conscious moments and perhaps little susceptible to academic investigation.

Perhaps all this would not appear so odd to Africanists, students of musical creation or comparative anthropologists. But for rationalist researchers – still the majority, I fancy – it must seem like some kind of fraud or, at best, a suspicious case of plagiarizing.

Conclusion

I in no way retract the emphasis on performance that has brought so much illumination to our understanding of language and speech. From this viewpoint Chomsky's more speculative, abstract, judgemental, acultural and mentalist analysis based in a theory of generative grammar and structure is not only unattractive (the main reason I think why many of us rejected it) but inconsistent with the evidence. But I have also come to believe that his view of language (language, not speech) as cognitive, in the mind, something there prior to its physical expression also has something to commend it. I now see that text as well as performance, competence as well as physical utterance have something to be said for them.

Both perspectives now seem to me fundamental for our understanding of language. Each needs to be given their due credit. Both need to be brought into play – a sports metaphor again – for a full grasp of what it is to possess that wonderful gift of human language, human expression and multisensory human performance.

8

Poem and story: The arts of dreaming and waking to sweet words

This chapter, in poetic and personal language, sketches some pertinent dimensions to such subjects, illustrating them with reference both to the comparative work on the subject and by reverting to a personally experienced case study – unusual, or is it? – which presents a challenge to linguistic research and analysis.

Dreamed language: What is it?

I start off by again wondering about the origin of language. If it was not the result of blind evolutionary forces or deliberate creation or somehow from 'when the ape came down from the trees and needed to communicate' (a pretty tale) – then how? And more pressingly, from *where*?

The subject in certain of its dimensions attracts immense interest and in some ways a vast literature surrounds it with a constant stream of compilations and commentaries. A series of literary, historical and anthropological studies have examined aspects of the use or collection of language in particular places or periods – and, especially, of quoted language from the generated heritage of the past; linguists and philosophers have engaged in technical analyses; literary and cultural scholars have developed a variety of approaches to allusion, citation or creativity; and the topics of inter-textuality, originality and appropriation have become a focus of interest to, among others, cultural historians, educationalists and postmodernist scholars. But amid this profusion there seemed no direct treatment of the questions teasing me: about just how language and imagination are linked and constructed as a human talisman and, above all, how such a wondrous gift could have arisen in the first place.

The question demands a wider perspective. The conventional ethno-graphic viewpoint privileges a short-scale, local focus. So too, surprisingly, do studies of the Chinese or the ancient classical world where I tried to contextualize contemporary snapshots by a longer vision. For though there is now some general interest across the better-informed social sciences in psychiatric perspectives and 'the imaginary', much is still aligned towards the hard sciences rather than the 'liquid' and dreamed knowing that demands exploration.

Like the beautiful jade pendant given me by my husband, language is at once carved-out and natural, from the material world but created by human hand, a precious heirloom from the past, in a way eternal but shaped by earthly love. How much we owe to that small human band, the first. How could language, like them, not have been formed just the once? And if, as now seems agreed, there was just one original human group destined to spread in amazing ways across Africa, across Europe and, before the breakage of continents, into Australia and the Americas, carrying, as we anthropologists know so well, their cultural heritage with them, how could language, that originary imaginative creation of speech, not have travelled with them?

Consider the beauties of poetry and verbal art. Whence could have come the sonnet form, or Shakespeare's play with it? Surely he found it, then used it in his artistry of words, sparked – is it over-romantic to see this as the eternal human ingredient? – by love.

Or the rhymes and rhythms, already there, with which, from outside herself, the poet is inspired? When I wrote – no, was given – a poem as the sun rose over the beautiful Hauraki Gulf and its surrounding mountains, I did not search for rhymes, they were there waiting for me. The form was waiting too – I did not know until later that it was a sonnet of kind, even if it *did* end up as 15 lines!

> *Through mountain dawn and gentle breeze*
> *By starstream lit and breaking heart*
> *O'er highland pass and tossing seas*
> *To seek again by craft or art*
> *A love long caught and scattered fine*
> *In dust and spume and foam of grieve-*
> *-ing heartbreak, in the sands of time ...*
> *Left here to weep and sink amid*
> *Tsunami billows, lost, a-fear'd*
> *Where love's once gleaming joy was hid.*
> *Alas it's left me, lone and drear*
> *With heart and self adriften'd, dear'd*
> *Oh come my love, my only dear*
> *In scattered winds, my once-loved whole*
> *My heart, my self, my only soul.*
> (Auckland, 28 March, as the morning star faded into the dawn)

The same was so of a later verse about a close friend's loss, much wept-over, arriving with me between sleep and waking in June 2012. Here was no rhyme (mostly – I was not conscious of what there was till much later) but with rhythm and cadence already in place when I looked to write it down the next day.

> *You have been given a great gift.*
> *The gift of steadfastness to see her die*
> *love to hold her through the night*
> *and close her eyes.*
> *sorrow to see her gone*
> *courage to travel the hard death road with her*
> *and then without her*
> *impossible courage – to return*
> *return to those who called you,*
> *braveness to live alone,*
> *fortitude to find your friends*
> *and Friends, again,*
> *grief and pain and more-more pain*
> *living a lone soul's earthly life,*
> *light of the ocean*
> *beloved wife*
> *star of the sea, for aye.*
> (quoted by permission of the dedicatee)

We humans have resources, handed down from our ancestors, for the generating and utterance of beautiful poetic and loving words. As the ancients knew well, here is a miraculous gift, from the past, from the creation of the seers and poets of old.

From where comes this wondrous resource in the first place? Whence the origin of the generated miracle of language? A question indeed. How can we know?

One person's experience

For me? I have found creative, created, literature in my dreams. I do not know the name, the place, the time. But I know it is somehow from beyond myself, outside even of earthly mortal creation. But without our human creativity, our very own action, our very selves, it could never have come to be. This must seem – as it does, indeed, to myself – the product of religious or mystical ideologies, paranormal, hallucinatory; certainly not the scientific hard evidence expected of linguistic analysis. And yet ... it is indeed language-in-use, perhaps more commonly occurring than we realize and certainly recognized by the ancients (see for example Harris 2007) – not to be denied just because it has seldom been fully described or taken seriously.

So let me move now to my dreams and their outcomes – or rather my 'Dreams', or what I have come to refer to as 'power dreams' – a very personal experience. And yet, like others engaged in reflexive anthropology, reported for what others can or might make of them.[1] The dreams are not so much 'miraculous' (though 'gift' and 'miracle' are apt descriptions). This example is an authentic one and not, to my surprise too, in any way a hoax. It is also an experience new to me, now approaching my 80th year, and to many will seem deluded (though less so, I will claim, than my later experience of telepathic communication – on which more in another place [Finnegan 2012]). But if so, it is a sustained delusion, a kind of myth of symbolic worth, true, I believe, to itself. Remember also that anthropologists, and linguists too, have long held a reputation for giving credence, *pro tem* at least, to the beliefs and language practices they find, and listen to them tenderly.

The stories that then followed on my dreams came as I visited, unplanned, a dream world of others' experiences – my own too, and those of my culture.

Transformed into words they carried, no question, that familiar narrative experience of human living, the form in which we shape our lives and being – a form in which, perhaps not fortuitously, I already had an interest (Finnegan 1967, 1998; see also Bauman 2004). Over the last few months, since a neurological illness in the summer, stories have been told to me, unexpected, unsought, in a series of dreams, later viewed, differently, as a series of quasi-visions revealed between sleeping and waking. They existed already – as do, miraculously, the events and practices of the field, situation for field-researchers: waiting there for me, for us. They were there before I knew it: independent of my thoughts or actions, enlarging as I struggled, as in the field, to note and record them and as my observations grew, uncovering themselves before my watching eyes.

They came so fully formed that I sometimes wondered if they were truly mine or plagiarized from another's hand (readers are welcome to their own interpretations: I am after all interested in quotation as well as dreams). Anthropologists and sociolinguists will scarcely be surprised to hear that much was generated in the culture of present and past literary creation and its artful words – and, as I know well, its familiar sights and sounds.

But I know that ultimately my dreams do not come directly from any of those – unless perhaps from some unknown hand in some other century or

1   The anthropological analysis of dreams and dreaming is limited. Relevant works include, among a few others, Abraham 1979, Basso et al. 1992, Bulkley et al. 2009, Burke 1997, Devereux 1969, Edgar 1995, 1999, 2000, 2003, 2004, 2008, 2009, 2011, Harris 2009, Jedrej and Shaw 1992, Kracke 1987a, b, 1994, Lohmann 2003, Tedlock 1986; allied to this are the stimulating if often challenging insights of psychologists, chief among them of course Freud and Jung. Recently there has been some revival of interest, going along with the increasing interdisciplinary focus on psychotherapy, practical prophecy and self-help manuals, many of them now on much-consulted pages on the web.

galaxy past or to come. My trade is words and listening to words, so I have worked, hard, at revising and crafting the tales and how they might sound in the reading. This could be painful, though sometimes more in the later reading than the first writing; funny too, especially some of God's antics (I hope they don't offend) and parts of Sophy's story in Farrar 2012a – to tell the truth I rather hope they do offend university folk (more likely and equally good they'll make them laugh). All in all it has been a surprisingly happy experience transforming my power dreams into verbal narrative.

The stories came as visually communicated scenes fully formed, gradually unveiled as I walked further in that strange land. Not dynamic, as is the way of language, or at that stage narrative, they were static tableaux rather than dreams in the usual – narrativized – sense. Things fell gradually into place as I learned their detail: Anne the defrauded mother – only after I had written the small scene in *The Little Angel* when Fionnuala brings her child did I realize that he was Anne's own son; and that she was also St Anne who comes not in nativity scenes but with her own recent-born son in Virgin-and-Child pictures. Francis and his birds, and Athene's grey eyes (born fully formed from the head of Zeus, I recall) also came later. And Sophia – by day in Sir Wulfram's cottage (her nights have not been shown to me): I need not after all have been so exercised about whether palace sleeping arrangements would permit Corin and Fionnuala's eventual union.

And the little cat – it was only late on that I noticed him (except he was all the time a she!), hiding behind the coal scuttle in God's study as he and Sophia talked wisdom together, trying to overhear them so as to pass it on, suitably edited, to her kittens. Unlike God, she hadn't had a private education or learnt Latin (God said it didn't matter but she knew better: wisdom might not be everything – she knew that well from chasing the palace mice – but even in heaven it was something!). Near the start of Sophia's story the cat had all the time been chasing sunbeams in the corner, it was just that I hadn't looked that way. So too with the scene when she leapt to Sophy's so-unexpected rescue. My sympathy for her came late, for though I knew that story ended in her redemption, I wrote it unwillingly.

The first intimation came one or two years ago (I don't recall exactly when – was it the hidden start of my now-recovered illness?) when I saw the dream-vision that ended that first four-stage tale: the most powerful experience of them all, and one that remains strongly with me. In it I saw a vivid image of two cloaked figures (male I think, perhaps angels, or maybe God and Christ – even dreams, as anthropologists well know, are shaped by cultural traditions), bending over a motionless body on the ground at the top of the grassy slope. I know it is Sophia's and also mine too, also at the same time Soa's and Sophy's (the other dimensions of 'wisdom') even as they struggle up the slope and are weighed in the balance. The little angel stands on one side: their conscience, I think, less tender than the more understanding advocate sitting opposite. The winged figures repeat tenderly, in words with overtones for most Western readers, Christian or other, of the wonders and dangers – and unavoidable necessity – of humans' free will:

> *Why should she not walk where she wants?*
> *What matter if she loses her way?*
> *Are we not here to bring her home on our shoulder*
> *And lead her in the soft primrose glades*

The pain is unbearably there too – violence, war, the cross. By the end God bitterly regrets creating men and women, and snakes and apples, the scene with which the story began. But he eventually decides it was right, for all the pain, above all that of his dear son (Mary wasn't of so much account – quite helpful, spiritual, but only a girl!). He realizes he has to go through that pain of creation and its results again, and again, and again. And that only humankind, not himself, can ever end it despite all the emails carrying his love stories that he eventually manages, with the help of the younger generation, to dispatch through the ether.

Next – and while, I think, I was already into my period of illness when I found myself unable for a time to voice the words in my mind – I perceived the dreamlike experience, out of normal consciousness, as representing not so much heaven as a setting of passive acceptance, as I had pictured it, or of listening to already-perfect heavenly choirs (I am after all a [rather poor] choral singer myself) but of widening and deepening experience, both known and untried. That image does not figure directly in the stories but forms their background. And the last dream tableau for that first story (Farrar 2012a) – the folding of Francis and Sophia in the safety of his wings followed by his betrayal and his gift – is the pivot of the whole, and (with some help from the angel and the little cat) gives structure to the overall narrative.

We also see the angel developing from an anxious little figure into something more like the senior experienced personalities he'd secretly hoped to emulate (ideally St Michael whose trumpet, perhaps mistakenly, he secretly coveted). He was one of those few who learned from participating not just (as he was supposed to) by standing back: he too easily became the participant, not just the observer (was this a reflection of the tensions, not fully appreciated at the time, of the field-working participant-observer, anthropologist or linguist?). Perhaps he had read Aeschylus, though I doubt if ancient Greek tragedy was on his syllabus, for his experience again recalls those strains of detachment together with participation.

Gradually, as in Greek drama, the angel learns from suffering, his own and others', and grows older in wisdom and experience. Some might think, with me, that he was excessively tender to Sophia, the Virtuous One of the three wisdoms (if he'd taken 'The Virgins' option in the heavenly Diploma programme, he reflects, he might have coped better and noticed her failings, but it had sounded too scary!). But with his foundation in Transferable

Skills he was quite good on Soa the self-trumpeting slut, specially on her Witchiness which he focused very hard on recording for St Peter and the heavenly archivists. He was less good on other dimensions so she got away with a lot. In the end he makes not too bad an overall assessment, and at least her 'sins' were properly recognized ones: on St Peter's list.

He had more trouble with Sophy (originally Sāfia but she wasn't going to accept someone else's identity, was she!). There hadn't been a Feminist module on offer, or if there was he had accidentally-on-purpose missed it, so was a bit lost. He wasn't so bad at spotting the bluebells that she'd wanted to pick and so destroy or, more obvious, the music, and warmed to her childhood aspirations. But he'd been brought up to respect Authority so was flummoxed. He couldn't find any proper 'sins' (he'd also been frightened off the Advanced Terran Crime diploma, but why hadn't his tutors warned him about the confusions allowed on earth?). Yes he knew St Judas had kept telling him with that twinkle that Sinning was more complicated than the elementary syllabus made out, and Job would do a little dance and agree. He was planning to take the 'Sinn-ology Theory' course sometime ('the Sink') – rather a demanding module, he'd heard, and he hadn't come across anyone who'd stayed the whole way. He'd opt for the 'Theory' dissertation of course, distance mode – he'd had enough of the in-service bit. He went on being confused by Sophy and only finally got through with the help of the little cat's leap and, to his surprise, his trumpet.

Without consciously thinking about it, I too had been dissatisfied with Sophy (the activist-feminist)'s ending. The little cat saved her eventually – late to appear (cats don't come to order, don't you know!) – but it was only on a sleepy autumn morning in late September that I saw that an angelic trumpet player had already fixed it and on a later night that I saw that God's boredom and the creation of free will was both the beginning and end.

In the concluding section, the angel's little sister peeps in, tut tuts at the tumbled bedclothes, and rescues the trumpet just starting to slip off the bed. She takes away his filthy wings to wash. We only get a glimpse (that comes in the third tale), just a fleeting impression of a mischievous character who gets away with anything and is adored by her big brother who in the end is prepared to sacrifice everything for her.

By the end the once-little nervous angel has got more ambitious and wonders about the programme on Higher Design they were hoping to put Steve Jobs onto when he'd recovered from his unapple-y bumpy trip to heaven. They were in a hurry, for by now it was past time for them to catch up with the latest technology and extra-territorial comms. But – typical! – open only to A* Star students.

The three Sophias were of one womb but separated by the experiences of their lives – or perhaps by successive incarnations and by their contrasting, up to a point chosen, routes to heaven. They are finally united, in death. I was reminded by this that in many African narratives the heroes are twins (sometimes three twins), chained in life but not, I presume, in death, and endowed with the 'four eyes' that give them insight into the spirit world.

Given the tradition in which I grew up, and the biblical and Bunyan-rich Quaker school I attended, the language, cadences and images of the narratives cannot avoid being biblical, though in ways I was not aware of when I was writing them down – sometimes, as it felt, from dictation. I worked, hard, at trying to put the dreams into the narrative language in which I grew up, influenced by I know not how many novels, both high- and low-brow, that I read before sleeping (sleeping – I begin to see the connection). The dreams themselves came, as I say, as static non-narrative tableaux, not linguistic, so transforming them in story was a work of art, drawing on crafts I had spent my life polishing. The voice I came to develop was at first (as one perceptive friend observed) uncertain and uneven, but eventually clear and sustained.

What I failed to realize at the time – as with so many elements in these stories – was that Sophia, my heroine, was also in some sense the Virgin Mary, and Francis the Father God who Zeus-like exploited as well as loved the daughters of earth, fathering his sons upon them and cuckoo-like passing them on to others to rear. The whole might be called a religious-Christian allegory – except that 'allegory' gives too literal an interpretation – 'myth' might be a better term for these stories. Like so much lyric poetry and narrative they were also in a yet deeper sense – and again I failed to recognize this until I read them, complete – ultimately about myself.

The pictorial images in my eventual texts came later – or rather the illustrations that I found for them, not through my dreams directly but following their inspiration and thus discovering them in Google. They added a deeper meaning, symbolic, grasping at reality, in the way words cannot do. This symbolic dimension was markedly there in the merging of the three Sophias (at the end of Farrar 2012a) but also with flashes elsewhere. There was the dazzling Envoy, the instant when Soa suckles her child and looks forward so vainly and pathetically to family life, or Sophy's brief glimpses of beauty, even her lukewarm kindness to the old king and, later, to Fionnuala and Corin – but not Sophia's union with Corin: their love was mortal, not eternal. Much else has gradually emerged from the strange mist-shrouded land of my fieldwork between sleeping and waking.

The stories then, like an anthropologist's perceptions in the field and, indeed, like language and communication, are, as I had glimpsed earlier (2002), strikingly multidimensional. They can only be fully realized, perhaps, through the full sensorium of sounds and touches and sights – landscape, sea and sky; birds both strong and weak (devouring eagle as well as 'my little thrushlet'); trees and their traceries of branches; wild flowers and their fragrances; streams and still waters – and the glowing light of pearl catching pearl, threatening sword dazzling eyes, whirling timeless skies and great oceans, the pain of birth, separation, and sacrifice. And the breeze ever so gently stirring the cloaks of the two forms, bringing comfort and understanding at the heart of the first narrative.

I wrote down the stories (not 'up', I now realize) while they were still fresh for fear the vision might fade, most lately the Prelude which arrived on the night of 29 September, further extended into God's Creation and Design in late October, and finally (finally I hope), the little cat's role, more central than I could possibly have imagined at the outset (strange – I am not a cat person!). By now I am also intrigued by the at-first undifferentiated all-encompassing devils gradually getting transformed into shaped attacking demons with a name, a label – those quintessential entities of linguistics – and a means of capture and control, finally separating into a confrontable and quietening (but thankfully for human will and personhood, never fully conquered) external and visible Dragon, to be further personalized in the final tale of what has now become, as dictated by my dreamed list, Catherine Farrar's 'Self Quartet'.

The words sometimes still expand in my dreaming and waking – but not in mortal time as my clock winds backwards. Anthropologists, of all people, are sceptical of the boundaries between fantasy and reality so will not be surprised that the stories are clear and present in my memory. They are abidingly true and real, given to me to reveal through my own imperfect voice.

The scenes were often balletic as I dreamed them, pictorial and stylized tableaux, taking me beyond the here and now. This was especially so in the 'United' act as the king enfolds Sophia majestically in his cloak and on a breath lays them softly down and Francis's deep bass dissolves into the Sanctus from Bach's *B Minor Mass*. That scene came early and was among the most powerful, one of the central narrative cores.

I have come to realize, from direct reflection on the puzzle and from/ in my dreams earlier, that the words I draw on to transform my wordless dreamed tableaux, and then my crafted words, into stories are giving me a glimpse of a milky fluid way made up of the gathered created constellations that they are set into the universe. It is as if the sky and edges of my brain wherein they reside – or rather float, and that I must select from, are making up the words and stories: they start from constellations of stars as it were, imagined and real, drawn into images and then, later, my words. And all those beautiful words from throughout the universe and the centuries, and the precious prayers that circulate and cultivate the globe of our – and my own – existence. Not the least of these experiences is the emotion that someone should be speaking prayers for me, and the lullabies and cradling in my mother's womb. Fanciful? And yet this is now the lived experience of my narrative language uses. Is this the beginning of human verbal creation?

Music

Music came later. That surprised me at first as I had always seen music and cadence as, if anything, prior to and underlying speech. But perhaps indeed it does lie deeper and my imagination had, unknowing, to dig further. The carol in the story is one I have sung and loved since we sang it in a wonderful four-part choir during my schooldays.

The angel Gabriel from heaven came ...
Most highly favoured lady

Gloria

I woke one morning with it in my head and was amazed how, as with so much else, it was already there in the tales. The lovely hymn 'Amazing Grace' came later but even more powerfully, with its wonderful locally composed words (were they dreamed too?) and its negro-spiritual melody (see http://www.sheetmusicplus.com/title/Amazing-Grace/19410846).

Amazing grace! how sweet the sound
That sav'd a wretch like me!
I once was lost, but now am found
Was blind, but now I see. ...
The earth shall soon dissolve like snow,
The sun forget to shine;
But God, who call'd us here below,
Will be forever mine.
(John Newton, 1779)

It was constantly there in the background, the words coming through audibly by the end.

And there, later, were the words and tune of the 'Three Kings' carol ('Three kings from orient lands afar') which I woke with one morning during an autumn Dartmoor holiday, as so often between dream and waking. My first reaction was that here at last was an irrelevant piece, hoping indeed it would prove so: I resented its apparently glib intrusion and the labour of introducing it. But that too turned out to belong to the story; it was just that I hadn't seen it before.

And then I found myself drifting up from deep sleep one cold dawn with *Deo gratias* ringing in my head. Unwinding its words backwards, I found the long-sung traditional fifteenth-century 'Adam lay ybounden' with its near-heretical conclusion, words and tune that usually I think about only at Christmas. Again it seemed at first irrelevant, but I soon realized, sleeping and waking through the rest of that night, that it was in Soa (the vixen harlot)'s story which before had seemed, though completed, so thin and uninteresting. And I saw that the 'Blessed be the day / That apple taken bin', with its stunning and, to me, new theological message, was after all central to the tales. How could I have known that or transferred it into verbalized text without inspiration from some external (or unconscious?) source?

The abiding theme of the whole, then, is both musical and verbal, prime among the expressive arts of our culture. For me and for the stories this was the more resonant for the local associations of the erstwhile slave-trader composer of the words, and the African connections of the tune, both deeply expressive for my own personal – but shared – background.

Whence come these earthly heavenly arts?

Can it be that here is some original form of language, denied in our waking hours but recovered and recoverable in song and dream? Listen to the beautiful declaimed words of lovely poetry, think of Shakespeare's or Elizabeth Barrett Browning's love poems: can they be seen to originate in the trial-and-error endeavours of earthly concerns? Or the sonnet form itself? Petrarch hardly constructed it from nothing – so where did he find it? Cannot dreams and imagination be seen as, whatever the proximate causes, the ultimate generating force of human language?

There may still be more stories and songs – sequels with some of the very same characters – waiting to show themselves as I wake from sleep and dream. And might such an experience – not mine alone, but the many instances given us in our literature – not give us pause to consider new insights into the nature and processing of language? A talisman, like my jade pendant, wrought by men's hands, a product of the earth and of art – but surely – metaphorically if you prefer – of divine origin?

9

Where is literature?

What is the existential status of what we call 'literature' and how is it differentiated from other art forms? Can we be sure what we are talking about in our facile references to the literary? In a challenging article that starts not from the conventional Western literary canon but from traditional Japanese theatre, Andrew Gerstle has suggested that the concept of 'performance literature' might be illuminating as an analytic and comparative tool when approaching the literatures of Africa and Asia (Gerstle 2000: 43). This chapter follows up his approach, seeing it as relevant not just for Africa or Asia but also for any verbalized forms in which performance has a part and thus for our theories of 'literature' more generally.

It is a set of issues worth tackling. For despite the now-accepted problematizing of the concepts of 'text' and 'literature', conventional approaches to studying literature and literary theory still seem to bypass performance and to start from the position that the defining focus is 'literary texts', prototypically texts in writing, and that this is how and where literature exists. Most textbooks and glossaries on literature contain little or nothing about the complex performed aspects of literature in the sense of its realization as public enacted display in the here and now. The ramifications of the familiar notion by which, say, a display of African story-telling, a poetry recital or the production of a Nô drama are examples of performance in a way that, say, a theological treatise or a written libretto are not (on the face of it anyway) – these seem to have little visibility in the standard accounts of literature.

It is perhaps scarcely surprising that scholars have conceived of 'literature' as basically existent in written texts. After all, we have long accessed past literary enactments – across centuries, sometimes millennia – through the medium of verbalized texts-on-a-written-page. This is what exists, it seems. Non-verbalized and non-writable performance dimensions, ephemeral and elusive, could not be captured or directly transmitted from the past, and therefore could be passed over as without any abiding graspable reality. The written verbal formulation, something hard and permanent, appeared

as the essence, a notion further reinforced in some languages by the association of 'literature' with alphabetic writing (letters). As a standard reference
book has it, 'at its most neutral, and broadest, literature signifies textual
manifestations of writing' (Wolfreys et al. 2002: 51). Or, more explicitly,
in a statement that would probably be implicitly accepted by many, Peter
Widdowson defines literature as written works, by which he means 'works
whose originating form and final point of reference is their existence as
written textuality' (Widdowson 1999: 15). Literature must therefore must
be 'reproducible in print', and:

> A centrally determining characteristic of 'the literary' … is that it is
> realised in a tangible object which is readily present for close inspection
> or re-reading, and that it does not have to be performed (or pre-emptively
> interpreted) in order to be read for the first time as unmediated text.
> (Widdowson 1999: 127, 128)

The notion of performance might seem to lie outside this ground of
literature, even be opposed to it. Indeed those that have pointed to the
significance of performance have been less the literary scholars than
anthropologists, folklorists, cultural historians, ethnomusicologists, and
other scholars (and practitioners) coming to the issues from first-hand
experience of performance arts, especially of forms outside the conventional
high-art Western canon. These have now joined with perspectives linked to
the continually developing genres of popular culture and from the growing
acknowledgement of the wealth and reality of non-Western literary forms.
This chapter, then, attempts to take up Gerstle's challenge by some direct
consideration of the concept of performance in the context of literature.
How, if at all, does literature exist in performance? What has 'performance'
to tell us about literature and literary theory? How is it related to text?
And can we best appreciate the literary forms of some Asian and African
cultures – in some ways paralleling, in others apparently very different from
those of the West – by recognizing them as 'performance literatures'?

Literature and 'performance'

One way into tackling these questions has been through the notion of oral
forms of literary expression. From some viewpoints this has never been
contentious. The Homeric epics (in some sense at least 'oral'), Elizabethan
lyrics, performed poetry, folk tales, scripts for or from plays – all these have
long been presented as written formulations, studiable as literary texts. The
next step however is more important: looking directly at the oral-ness of
such examples as a positive and essential quality. Through the so-called
'orality' studies that have developed in various guises, mainly from the

1960s onwards, it has become increasingly clear that an oral performance can be analysed not just as the contingent setting for some abiding – writable – text but as itself the central reality. There is now a large body of scholarship focusing on concepts like 'oral', 'orality', 'oral literature' or 'orature', concerned among other things to understand oral performance in its own right.

One consequence has been to extend the concept of literary expression to include many unwritten forms and, equally significant, to treat their orally performed qualities as part of their literary realization. South African Xhosa praise poetry for example, declaimed in reverberating and unmistakable style by the praise singer, inspires its listeners through acoustic effects – rhythms, sonic parallelisms, strained mode of articulation, intonations and ringing praise names (Opland 1998) – while the sophisticated artistry of Limba oral narrative in Sierra Leone lies not just in verbal content but in the vivid way the narrator voices the performance and the skilful use of vocal dynamics, tempo and intonation. Oral genres from throughout the world once dismissed as crude and 'pre-literate', from Mongolian oral epics or the lyrics of Indian love songs to the extensive unwritten performances of Africa, have now come to be analysed as forms of literature – of 'oral' literature.

Once we lift our gaze from the written texts alone, it also becomes clear that oral delivery is in fact a much more 'normal' and frequent occurrence in the world's literary experience than we would imagine from the conventional closures of English literature studies. In medieval Europe, for example, written texts did indeed exist, but public oral delivery rather than private reading was the typical mode of literary realization (see for example Coleman 1996). Oral performance of poetry was fundamental to literary experience at the Japanese Imperial court, and recitation was the predominant mode for Japanese narrative more generally (Gerstle 2001).

Nor is this so only in the past or outside Europe. English poetry performances take place in schools, pubs, colleges, halls and other public places (Middleton 2002), while in American clubs and coffee houses 'slam' performers compete in their scintillating manipulation of the arts of oral poetry, with rhyme, alliteration, coded gestures and 'electric and continuous exchange between poet and audience' (Foley 2002: 5). The concept of performed oral literature has opened up a more generous understanding of the diversities of literary realization, taking us beyond the narrow notion of written texts and offering a whole new range of material for the comparative student of literature.

This recognition of the positive features of oral literary forms admittedly sometimes led to some exaggeration of their significance and distinctiveness. It seemed for a time as if one single process had been revealed that covered all oral composition. Elements of the foundational Western myth sometimes intruded too: of a fundamental divide between oral and written, with a binary opposition between two contrasting types of social and cognitive organization: the one oral, communal, emotional, non-scientific, traditional, primitive; the other literate, rational, scientific, individualistic, creative, civilized, Western, modern. This made it easy to fall into the assumption that in those cultures – or genres or situations – where oral performance was significant, the literary forms would similarly be more communal, collective or emotive, etc. than for the conventional forms of 'normal' – written, Western – literary texts.

By now most scholars with any experience outside the parochialities of modern Western culture would question the attempt to take as universal that powerful Enlightenment vision of Western history and destiny that invokes the rationality of language together with fundamental divisions among humankind tied to the presence or absence of (alphabetic) writing. Instead they would point (as in this volume) to the existence not of a single 'orality' but of multiple forms of oral expression, to be found in the urban contexts of today no less than 'far away and long ago'.

Further, contrary to what was once believed, not all oral literature rests on the mix-and-match variability of creative composition in the moment of delivery. That is one form, well attested in the Yugoslav epic poems studied by Parry, Lord and other scholars in the 'oral-formulaic' tradition. But there are also cases of prior composition and of exactly repeated delivery. Martin Orwin describes the unwritten 'definitive texts' of some Somali poetic genres, for example, with their qualities of exact repeatability and copyright which in a sense stand outside the moment of delivery and have their own abiding reality (Orwin 2003). So too with some oral poetic genres in Oceania, where the words of songs were composed in advance and great pains taken to ensure exact reproduction as they were rehearsed and eventually performed by choral singers. There is not just one form of oral literary realization but many different arrangements along a continuum of more, or less, crystallized and stable oral texts.

Nor is there just one relation between the 'performed oral' and the 'textual written' or always a clear distinction between them. Writing can interact with oral performance in many different ways, for example as performance score, dictated transcription, crib sheet, memory cue, prompt book, notes for a speech, printed version of a memorized poem or of one composed orally, aid to help audiences to understand a performance as it develops, transcript to recreate and preserve memories of a performance, and multiple possible combinations of all of these or more. Ardis Butterfield (2002) illustrates how refrains in thirteenth-century French romances move between oral and written, performed and read, and there are plentiful cases ranging from Japanese court poetry or European classical and medieval examples of oral/aural delivery to contemporary pop lyrics, radio and television, where specific textual formations shift back and forth between oral and literate modes and can partake of both. The relation may change over time too or develop dynamically.

Daniel Meyer-Dinkgräfe comments on the phases of the transformative process from written text to performance as it comes out in the sequential phases creating theatrical performance. At first performers:

> read their lines from the text (script) in front of them, but by a certain stage in the rehearsal process, no further progress is possible while the performers still have the script in their hands. They need to take the big leap of speaking their lines from memory, without the script in their hands, at first perhaps supported by a prompt, but more and more having to rely in their memory within the framework set by the world of the play itself. Losing the security of the script makes the performers initially very vulnerable ... [and] temporarily weakens their portrayal of the character(s) they have to play. (Meyer-Dinkgräfe 2003)

Written and oral forms in practice often shade into each other and are related in manifold and variegated ways rather than existing as clearly distinctive modes or hard-edged properties.

With all their controversies and multiplicities, the central insight from these studies of orality has been a far-reaching one: the notion that oral forms are not only comparable to written literature in the sense (at least) of being formulateable as written texts paralleling recognized written genres, but also have their own qualities in which performance and declaration aloud and to an audience are of the essence. This has rightly challenged the Eurocentric and high-art-focused view of literature and enabled a greater appreciation of the literary reality of many African and Asian forms as well as of popular genres outside the traditional European canon.

From 'oral text' to multimedia enactment

This recognition may not take us far enough, however. Indeed, too dedicated a focus on the concepts 'oral' or 'orality', illuminating as these are, can sometimes be counterproductive. It can lead to the implicit assumption that the crucial feature of literary performance is always its oral medium, that it is in its verbal delivery that we find the core of the performed literary realization.

Overemphasizing the 'oral' can be a route to implicitly retaining the model of literature as essentially constituted in written texts. Oral texts are treated as literature in that, and insofar as, they are writable: either literature in some qualified sense (orally performed, but acceptable as consisting of words that are in principle writable); or becoming eligible to be considered as literature proper once transformed into written text. Such approaches can enlarge but not radically unsettle the position that for something to be literature it has to be 'susceptible to reproducibility in print' (Widdowson 1999: 127) with its reality lying in the writable words.

A narrow focus on the 'oral' also means excluding other perhaps equally important elements of performance. In fact, many performances are not principally a matter of 'words' – or at any rate not just of words. Characterizing a performance as 'oral' may not give a full account of the multiform realization that is performance.

Those who create performed literary art do not just deploy words but also play upon the flexible and remarkable instrument of the voice to exploit a vast range of non-verbalized auditory devices of which those notated within our written literary texts – rhyme, alliteration, assonance, rhythm and acoustic parallelisms – are only a small sample. There are also, as described earlier, the subtleties of volume, pitch, tempo, intensity, repetition, emphasis, length, dynamics, silence, timbre, onomatopoeia, and the multifarious non-verbal ways performers can convey (for example) character, dialect, humour, irony, atmosphere or drama. And then there are all the near-infinite modes of delivery: spoken, sung, recited, intoned, musically accompanied or mediated, shouted, whispered; carried by single or multiple or alternating voices. Performers operate within constraints certainly – social, situational, generic – but some combination from this array of auditory (and for the most part unwritten) resources is commonly central to both generic convention and performers' individual artistry. To say 'oral' and look just to the (writable) words is only the start of a whole series of rich diversities.

It is not just a matter of audition. Performers can also draw on an amazing store of visual resources. We can instance the uses of gesture, of facial expression, eye glances, bodily orientation, demeanour, visible movements, dress, ornament, make-up. Material accoutrements like sceptres or microphones may enter into the act, or associated visual images and exhibits: flags, icons, pictures, stage sets, graphic displays. Touch and smell sometimes have a part too, not least the tactile as well as musical and rhythmic interrelations of danced and embodied movement. The spatial dimensions of 'oral' performances also bring their multiplex resonances: the physical setting and spatial arrangements, the proxemic relations between various participants, the auditory and echoic as well as visual overtones of the performed event.

Time and time again performances of literature turn out to be multidimensional rather than purely or essentially oral in the narrow verbal sense of that term. Literary forms we are accustomed to read as verbalized texts need to be reassessed as multisensory. As Rosalind Thomas among others makes clear, our texts of classical Greek lyric and choral poetry 'silent on the written page, were originally accompanied by the lyre and other instruments, and choral poetry was sung by a group … accompanied by dance' (Thomas 2003: 349). The instruments and details of performers and participants may differ in other settings – indeed literature is nothing if not culture and genre specific – but the same general point applies in multiple other cases also, something too easily forgotten by those of us socialized into a focus on the silent page. Here again the 'words' may make up only a small proportion of the sung and choreographed whole and there are commonly other partisans besides the page, the author and the silenced reader.

We must remember too that this may not just be a matter of one lead performer pouring forth words in a vacuum – a picture it is easy to presuppose if we assume the model of single-line written text – but of a performance where the audience too may be part of the full meaningful event. There can be multiple interacting performers and multiple partici-pants in overlapping roles who between them build the atmosphere and drama of the art as a displayed realization in actual space and time. They co-create the multidimensional and embodied performance.

It is in this complex of arts that performances have their existence: visual, kinesic, acoustic, proxemic, material, tactile, mobilized, embodied. They are realized in varying combinations and degrees depending on the conven-tions of occasion, genre and social expectations as well as on the creativities with which the participants tackle both their constraints and their oppor-tunities. Some have richer, more variegated mixes than others. But all are multiplex, for literary performance is in one way or another inescapably multidimensional. These rich multisensory features are not contingent on the concrete formulations of the verbalized text – that 'tangible object ... present for close inspection or re-reading' as Widdowson had it (1999: 127, 128): they are themselves a solid part of the action.

Performance – text – performance

This now seems to have re-driven a wedge between the bare single-line texts of 'normal' written/writable literature and the exuberant multimedia life of performance. Trying to translate live performance into written transcript is to shortchange its vital multidimensionality. Transferring a multifaceted enstaged enactment into the simplex medium of writing may capture one element – the writable words – but passes by those other elements in which it lives. Correspondingly, a written script is surely a very different creature from the performance(s) into which it may ultimately be transformed. The two modes of realization – their means of existence – are simply not commensurate.

This is a significant issue, in the past only too often brushed aside. Performed African narrations, for example, were 'reduced' to writing and treated as if the simplified texts that resulted had captured their reality. In ways now much more widely appreciated, a failure to take account of the multidimensional ontology of performance is to represent it, misleadingly, as something quite other from its true realization.

However three further considerations should be brought into the argument. First, the simplified contrast between performance – multisensory, dynamic – and written text – one-line, linear – misses the equally important fact that writing too is multimodal. The multisensory characteristics of writing are usually invisible to those accustomed to the model of 'the written word' as something abstract, mental and context-free, part of the tradition of literate rationality so often envisaged as prototypical of the high culture and destiny of the West. But a growing number of cross-cultural studies of literacy challenge this ethnocentric myth and bring out the multi-modality and materiality of writing.

We need only reflect critically on our own experience. In approaching a piece of 'writing' we attend to much else besides the lettered words themselves. The typographic format tells us at once whether it is to be read 'as poetry' or 'as prose'. Layout, spacing and orientation (non-verbal all) show how we should read the texts: as, say, dialogue, quotation, refrain, title, emphasis, start, finish – visually displayed features that are not themselves words and yet all pertain significantly to the literary art. Pictorial image, colour and the materiality of its display can enter in too. This is so even in the alphabetic systems familiar to the West, especially (but not only) in their calligraphic and religious efflorescences where writing is less an information tool than a visual display (well brought out in Tonfoni's aptly titled *Writing as a Visual Art* [1994]).

Even more striking are the visually and pictorially rich non-alphabetic writing systems of Meso-America or Asia. Japan, for instance, has a long history of the creation and preservation of literary texts as art objects, often with illustrations (Gerstle 2003); a Japanese poem exists not only as performed but also as physical object, realized through the calligraphy, the nature and colour of the paper, and the sketches that illustrate it: the poem is meant to be seen as material (Shirane 2001). Carpenter (2002) notes the 'traces of the brush' in the calligraphic arts of East Asia as the callig-rapher interacts creatively with the challenges of different writing surfaces, aspects of the literary display. Nowadays too we are becoming increasingly familiar with the multiplex potential of new typographies and of computer-decorated extravaganzas where colour, shape, icon and moving image play such a large part: visual arts where the boundary between picture, writing and graphic dissolves.

Writing has an acoustic side too. As we have seen, written texts can be – and quite often are – realized in being recited or read out, bringing home the interaction, even overlap, between the sonic and the visual. The literature of the classical and medieval worlds was often delivered aloud, while nowadays parents and teachers read to small children, pupils prove themselves in audible reading, and for many religious adherents the full import of sacred writings comes through auditory declamation as much as written text. Audio books and computer multimedia now increasingly blur the boundaries between sounded and visible text. Some sonic elements are directly conveyed in writing, like the visual indications of rhythm, rhyme or emphasis. Others are created through the reader's art, whether aloud or silently – for even 'silent' reading is in a sense 'performed' by the reader and, especially for poetry and dialogue, experienced acoustically through our 'inner ear'. The resonances of auditory speech come through in our literate experiences too, both in a general way and in acoustic echoes of the kind Peter Middleton describes (2002) as shaping later readings of a poem first heard in public performance. Musical associations, too, sometimes run through written formulations, from the musical resonances in written versions of early French romance refrains (Butterfield 2002) or a printed lyric that can also be a song, to the explicit 'musicalization' of certain literary narratives (Wolf 1999).

Even leaving aside the elements of touch or olfaction that sometimes play a part, it becomes clear that in its actual practice even alphabetic writing has to be seen as both material and multidimensional, a matter not so much of objective referentiality as of a mix of arts together with the overtones and multisensory intertextualities with which it is imbued. Other writing systems add to the range, each with differing potentials and practices for the visible display of particular features, such as the indications for musical or vocal delivery (as in some of the Japanese texts described in Gerstle 2001) or the pictorial presentation of colour, shape or movement. This complexity is enhanced too in the cultural variability of how people read and relate to writing, something that involves far more than just visibly fixed words or verbally informative content. Far from being 'unmediated text', as in Widdowson's statement (1999: 128), any form of writing – and of written literature – is full of media.

This then brings into question the initially clear contrast between multimodal performance on the one side as against unilinear unmediated print on the other. In specific cultural situations and conceptualizations, of course, particular formulations may indeed be displayed and conceived as distinct and contrasting realizations in time and space. But as analytic and cross-cultural concepts the boundaries between 'performance' and written/ writable 'text' dissolve. The multiplex resources for human expression – visual, musical, pictorial, kinesic, verbal, material, tactile, somatic – cut across what had once seemed a divide.

This leads to a second consideration. It is fair enough to point out the defects of simple-minded transfers between performance and written text, between oral (performed) literature and written version. But in practice such translations are constantly happening. They are not confined to contrived scholarly transcriptions (though these too are part of the scene) but include regular links and interchanges among the many different modes of literary realization.

Thus classical and medieval literature could be displayed through oral delivery, through multimedia theatre and in writing; Hausa literary forms in northern Nigeria were disseminated in parallel written and oral modes; Japanese court poetry was composed and appreciated orally but also circulated in writing and print; novels are read aloud or presented as 'audio books'. Similarly European ballads, songs and stories have been realized through varying media, both concurrently and sequentially: in writing, in print, in live sung or spoken performance, in broadcast and in electronic modes. A poem can be viewed in print, read aloud, sung in musical setting, taken down in dictation, recited from memory, embellished in beautiful illustrated format – and all of these accepted in at least some sense and some contexts as versions of the same thing.

To go back to Jamaican–Canadian dub poet Lillian Allen, note her reflection on her own experience of such transfers. She mostly enacts her poetry in wonderfully flamboyant multisensory ways, but like several other Caribbean poets, has also presented them in print:

> Because words don't (always) need pages, I have published extensively in the form of readings, performances and recordings. I have been reluctant to commit my poetry to the page over the years because, for the most part, these poems are not meant to lay still.
>
> As I prepared poems for this collection, I was required to 'finalize' pieces I had never imagined as final. Like a jazz musician with the word as her instrument, reading and performing these poems is an extension of the creative and creation process for the work. In some ways, I had to reverse this process to 'finalize' these poems for print; finding their written essence; pages do need words.
>
> These poems breathe, they are alive. Sit quietly with them, read them aloud or shout them in public places. (Allen 1993: Preface)

From there the printed versions became texts not just for silent reading and/or for memories of live performances but the base for yet further performance by others as well as herself. And they are visual literary exhibits too, for like other Caribbean 'performance poets' Lillian Allen exploits creative typographical formats, special spelling and crafted layout to realize her poetry as visual display. Such intermedial transformations, as they might be called, are in practice a regular part of literary experience and take place within as well as between cultures, languages, genres and presentational modes – sometimes well recognized and validated, sometimes contested and highly political.

The overtones from one form of realization seep into others. In a way no performance is unique for it carries memories not only of other performances but of other modes and re-creations. Where such transformations are regular and recognized their overtones can be evoked for many purposes. Though each case has to be considered within the accepted cultural conventions of its time, genre or participants, this basic experience is scarcely rare. Print, too, may carry sonic echoes of a sung acoustic performance: someone who has once heard a poem performed by Lillian Allen will surely always hear it in the printed book also. Scripts may be intershot with theatrical associations as they are variously used for private reading, prompts for learning, cues for action or re-creations of performances; Kabuki illustrations may both evoke memories and give a stimulus for future embodied enactments; multisensory memories can move back and forward between oral, written, pictorial or danced displays. 'Reproductions' of performances can be imbued with the sounds and sights of the events from which in a sense they arise, at the same time as forming a base for yet further realizations and exegeses, perhaps in different media, with the intertextualities – the multidimensional memories and associations – running variously through all of them.

There is no need to multiply examples, for such transformations, complex as they are, are a common feature of human life. Even if there is some clear divide between multiplex performance and written text, then this is at least a divide that is in one way or another bridged every day, and in varying and variously used transformations. The bridgings and the multiple media deployed to achieve them are dimensions we need to recognize rather than jumping to conclusions about the ontological priority of any one of the variegated forms of display.

This is complemented by a third point. Performance and text are not, after all, two independently existing entities or states, but complementary dimensions of literary realization. In a way, all instances of literature are double-sided: created in the magic moment of performance but also enlarged into or reverberating with something more abstracted, detachable from the flow. On the one hand, all literary displays can be experienced and conceptualized in terms of their immediacy, in the temporal moment. There is not just one settled way this happens. It can be through embodied enactment or public theatrical display, or, more subtly, through the enperformancing of a written text, the immediacy of the 'now' when the reader personally experiences and re-creates it – 'performs' it. Performance lives 'in the present' (Phelan 1993: 146). This can be a relative and sometimes elusive quality, partly dependent on intent and perspective rather than a clear-cut event. For even here the experience is likely to be imbued with memories and connotations beyond the immediate moment: as Elin Diamond put it, 'Performance, even in its dazzling physical immediacy, drifts between present and past, presence and absence, consciousness and memory'; every performance marks out a unique temporal space but also 'embeds features of previous performances' (1996: 1).

So as well as the performancing emergent in the present acts of the immediate participants, there is the other sense in which a literary realization also exists beyond that temporal moment, in a more or less externalized and, as it were, transcendent mode, and with at least some elements of reproducibility. This too can take many different forms – including, but not confined to, materialized written text – and is again a matter of degree. It might be relatively intangible, a potentiality for realization rather than a material artefact, yet still in some sense abstractible: for example the Somali 'definitive' and repeatable poem-texts (Orwin

2003) or the 'mental texts' which Lauri Honko (2000) sees as lying behind performers' ability to deliver lengthy epics. Shared conventions about the gestural or musical or endanced systems for particular genres can be known and transmissible even if not articulated in verbal terms; externalized too, though in a different way, are film or audio and video recordings. Or it may be a matter of more visual and tangible forms 'objectivated' in space, whether as written displays or as other material artefacts which in some sense encapsulate and parallel performance, like the Ashanti gold weights that represent proverbs or the visual images of dramatic characters or episodes in stories.

To the multiplexities of literary realization, we must add these aspects of existence in differing but perhaps overlapping and concurrent spatial and temporal modalities, intershot too with memories and intermedialities that both exist in, and go beyond, the here and now. We make assumptions about the prior ontology of either 'text' or 'performance' at our peril for these may be less separate things than shifting interpenetrating phases and dimensions. In this light it becomes difficult to work with a definition of literature which posits that the written text must count as the 'originating form and final point of reference' (as in Widdowson's comment quoted above [1999: 15]).

These minglings of arts run along multiple dimensions, then, as they are formulated in particular manifestations and realizations. Literary displays turn out to involve multiplex processes, a series of overlapping and inter-mingling modes and media, human usages, temporal moments and spatial incarnations. We would be wise in any given case to avoid prior preconceptions about which of these is the 'real' or 'original' literary display, whether in terms of media drawn on or of the specific nature of their exhibition in spatial or temporal terms, for these vary with cultural and generic ideologies as well as with occasion, context, intent, agents, timing and the complex associations and overtones participants bring to its experience. Rather than continuing to juxtapose 'text' and 'performance', it may be more illuminating to explore the varying ways that human draw on a multi-faceted spectrum of expressive resources and transformations to create their multisensory literary displays, imbued with degrees of both immediacy and permanence.

How is literature?

Where do literature, narrative, poetry and so forth come from and in what do they consist? Surely not just in and from their expression in performance but, as is well known in both literary and musical history (and also from my own recent experience detailed here), from dream and vision. At any rate, however clothed in cultural and generic garb, they often seem to spring from somewhere outside and beyond the ordinary doings of the day-to-day round – or perhaps, equally mysterious, from somewhere deep inside the self. Might this mean a different appreciation of the nature of literary art?

Does this mean that amid all this multiplexity the notion of 'literature' has dissolved? Are we left just with the multifarious and no doubt wonderful array of human expressive media and modalities but no viable idea of literature?

That would be to go too far. I believe that we *should* retain the concept of 'literature'– this is not an argument for collapsing the study of 'literature' into 'cultural studies'. But I suggest we should envisage 'literature' not as definable by reference to Western written genres, but as an umbrella notion that can embrace all those displayed forms and events in which verbal artistry in some way plays a significant part.

'Literature' in this light is a relative and plural concept. 'Verbal artistry playing some significant part' – that is a matter of degree. In some instances the verbal element may indeed be dominant (though it remains important not to jump to conclusions about its priority or assume it can be treated in isolation). In other cases – or for some participants, some occasions – words as such may indeed play a role but in some senses be subservient to music, rhythm or dance.

The lyrics of some contemporary rock songs, for example, are certainly verbally articulated but, as Simon Frith well argues (1998), the joys of embodied movement and excitement carry as much import for their partici-pants as the apparent messages of the lyric-words; we can recall too the Japanese playwright and theorist Zeami's insistence that in composing a Nô play the musical and theatrical structure and the dance patterns come first, the words later (Gerstle 2000: 9). West African Ewe funeral 'songs' are in part realized through drum patterns that do not convey actual words but speak in the language of drums (Burns 2003). In other cases still, as with Japanese Kabuki prints or classical Greek vase paintings depicting mythical episodes that also figure in Greek plays, the verbal element may work through evocations and associations as much or more than in direct presentation. Just where we set the boundary of 'literature' here becomes a matter of judgement.

Literature is thus seamless at the edges not just for all the well-hewn arguments about the canon, the 'aesthetic', or 'high' versus 'ordinary', etc., but also in any given case for how, and how far, verbal art plays a part; this varies with genre, situation, participants, cultural tradition, ideology. Alongside the other issues with which they deal, our theories of literature need also to recognize the problematics around the role and relative signifi-cance of its words within the multidimensional web in which they work.

A multidimensional view of literature reality is the more timely given the increasing spread and accessibility of modern audiovisual technologies. The prime materialized way for capturing the ephemerality of embodied speech and action might once have seemed to be the permanence and replicability of print, giving a privileged ontological status to the written word ('seemed' because it is surely only the linguistic bias of certain sections of Western tradition that has allowed us to downplay the relative permanence and, for many centuries now, repeatability of pictorial representation). But now that storing and transmitting sound, images and movement have become commonplace, an enhanced sensitivity to the realities of multimedia literary displays can scarcely be regarded as revolutionary.

Taking this more plural approach to literature gives a vantage point for comparison. How far are particular literary genres or displays realized in more, or less, visual and spatial form? Engestured, enverbalized, endanced? Enacted through a mixture of media, including material artefacts? Co-created by the joint or differentiated contributions of plural participants? Enacted at specific points in time and/or formulated as detachable from the flow of the moment?

Even what at first sight looks like a thoroughly verbal formulation (and perhaps conceptualized as such for some contexts or purposes) may in practice be shot through with acoustic resonances, visual images or material display – varying perhaps with differing participants or differing cultural expectations but nonetheless a significant part of the mix, so that these multisensory dimensions, rather than being 'extra-literary' or 'proto-literary', are an essential part of the full literary realization. In the literary art of the conventional Western canon – one marvellous tradition, but only one among many – one main emphasis has often been on visual display involving words being realized in spatial material form structured through visibly exhibited layout and typography; whereas what strikes an outsider about many Asian literary forms is their pictorial-cum-theatrical-spectacle and their association with physically embellished art objects – a somewhat different emphasis again from the musicalized, endanced and verbalized, rather than tangibly materialized, bent of African literary forms. But one no sooner attempts such generalizations than exceptions and qualifications abound, not least the persistent interactions between the manifold human forms of literary display across the continents and over the centuries. All one can say is that, first, such questions are worth asking, though perhaps more for particular genres and examples than for wide regions of the world, and second, that any analysis of literary forms needs to be sensitive to the multiple dimensions likely to be in play – these are part of the reality of literature.

Underlying the discussion in this chapter, as in the book as a whole, has been the rich idea of 'performance', the stimulus for alerting us to multiple aspects too little considered by the literary scholars and of greater comparative reach than the closures of 'literature' into 'written text'. As it has turned out, the concept of 'performance literature' may not after all correspond to some special category of literature, thus perhaps less illuminating as a cross-cultural analytic term than it seemed in prospect. This is partly because, as suggested earlier, all literature is in a sense 'performed'.

There are also, it seems, problems about a twofold model (whether phrased as written/oral, text/performance, written literature/performed literature) where the first term counts as 'normal' literature, the second as literature only in a qualified way. In practice it appears that, rather than two opposed categories, there are a multitude of ways in which creativity-cum-convention can be artfully realized through words intermingled with other media. In some cases written or spoken words may indeed be used to play a leading role, in others they may have some part but only as interwoven with, perhaps outranked by, dance, music, gesture, visual images, tangible artefacts; and it is only in and through this multisensory mediation that they reach their full realization. It is to the cross-cutting multiplexities and relativities of time, space, multiple participants, multiple media, rather than to some special class of 'literature', that the seminal concept of 'performance' can direct us.

Finally, let me both reiterate and qualify the case for retaining the familiar concepts of 'literary' and 'literature'. These concepts, together with the (English) terminology of 'words', 'the verbal' or 'the linguistic', do not and cannot altogether get away from culture-bound connotations. The same applies to the hidden assumption, prevalent in many Western scholarly sites, that the literary is somehow the 'top art'. An equally good approach, and one arguably more congenial to some cultural traditions, might have been to start from dimensions that transcend linguistic articulation, like, say, 'the musical', 'the danced/embodied', or 'the pictorial', and bring together a cross-cultural conspectus of how these realizations too involve a shimmering cross-cultural constellation of arts (which might or might not include the verbal in any given instance). But it is surely also reasonable to pursue the complementary perspective of adopting a comparative perspective on the literary displays of human art.

The verbal role in these variegated displays may indeed be elusive, relative and contested, and always need to be understood in its multidimensional framework. But the recognition of this multiplexity, far from undermining our study of the wonderful human artistries and practices of literature, in fact gives us a better handle on understanding the modes in which they exist. It makes it possible to get away from the idea that there is just one 'proper' (Western) form of literature with its essential reality lying in writable alphabetic texts, while retaining a commitment to the understanding and appreciation of the literatures of the world.

FURTHER READING

Background and reference

Asher, R. E. and Simpson, J. M. Y. (eds) (1994) *The Encyclopedia of Language and Linguistics*, Pergamon [a great reference work].

Bauman, R. and Sherzer, J. (eds) (1989) *Explorations in the Ethnography of Speaking*, Cambridge University Press.

Duranti, A. (ed.) (2001) *Key Terms in Language and Culture*, Blackwell.

Goffman, E. (1981) *Forms of Talk* University of Pennsylvania Press [a classic].

Mey, J. L. (2009) *Concise Encyclopedia of Pragmatics*, Elsevier.

Sapir, E. (1921) *Language. An Introduction to the Science of Speech,* Harcourt [old but still one of the best; currently (2014) available free on kindle].

Tracey, K. (ed.) (1999) 'Language and social interaction at the century's turn', special issue, *Research on Language and Social Interaction* 32 [worth dipping into to get the flavour].

Wolfreys, J., Robbins, R. and Womack, K. (2002) *Key Concepts in Literary Theory*, Edinburgh University Press.

Yule, G. (2014) *The Study of Language*, Cambridge University Press [an accessible introductory text].

Chapter 1 What is the art of language?

Bakhtin, M. M. (1986) *Speech Genres and Other Late Essays,* University of Texas Press [a classic].

Clark, H. H. (1996) *Using Language*, Cambridge University Press.

Duranti, A. (1997) *Linguistic Anthropology*, Cambridge University Press.

Finnegan, R. (2014) *Communicating. The Multiple Modes of Human Interconnection*, 2nd (expanded) edn, Routledge.

Foley, J. M. (2002) *How to Read an Oral Poem*, University of Illinois Press.

Gans, E. (1999) 'The little bang: The early origin of language', *Anthropoetics* 5, 1.

Gippert, J., Himmelmann, J. and Mosel, U. (eds) (2006) *Essentials of Language Documentation*, Mouton de Gruyter.

Harris, R. (1987) *The Language Machine*, Duckworth.

Chapter 2 Playing with the heroes of human history

Abraham, K. (1979), 'Dreams and Myths: A Study in Folk Psychology', in *Clinical Papers and Essays on Psychoanalysis*, Hogarth Press.

Bauman, R. and Briggs, C. L. (2003) *Voices of Modernity. Language Ideologies and the Politics of Inequality*, Cambridge University Press.

Boone, E. H. and Mignolo, W. D. (eds) (1994) *Writing Without Words. Alternative Literacies in Mesoamerica and the Andes*, Duke University Press.

Diringer, D. (1968) *The Alphabet. A Key to the History of Mankind*, 2 vols, Hutchinson.

Hodge, R. and Kress, G. (1993) *Language as Ideology*, 2nd edn, Routledge.

Chapter 3 'Artisting the self': A tale of personal story

Bruner, J. (2002) *Making Stories*, Harvard University Press.

Finnegan, R. (1998) *Tales of the City*, Cambridge University Press.

Linde, C. (1993) *Life Stories. The Creation of Coherence*, Oxford University Press.

Riessman, C. K. (1993) *Narrative Analysis*, Sage.

Chapter 4 Forget the words …: It's *performance!*

Allen, L. (1993) *Women Do This Every Day: Selected Poems of Lillian Allen*, Women's Press.

Bauman, R. (1992) 'Performance', in R. Bauman (ed.) (1992) *Folklore, Cultural Performances, and Popular Entertainment*, Oxford University Press.

Brown, S. (1987) 'Dub poetry: Selling out', *Poetry Wales* 22: 51–4.

Cooper, C. and Devonish, H. (1995) 'A Tale of Two States: Language, Lit/orature and the two Jamaicas', in S. Brown (ed.) *The Pressures of the Text: Orality, Texts and the Telling of Tales*, Birmingham University African Studies Series 4.

Finnegan, R. (2007) *The Oral and Beyond: Doing Things with Words in Africa*, James Currey.

Hymes, D. (1975) 'Breakthrough into Performance', in D. Ben-Amos and K. S. Goldstein (eds) *Folklore: Performance and Communication*, Mouton de Gruyter.

Hymes, D. (1977) *Foundations in Sociolinguistics: An Ethnographic Approach*, Tavistock.

Schechner, R. (1988) *Performance Theory*, Routledge.

Chapter 5 Reclothing the oral

Duranti, A. (1997) *Linguistic Anthropology*, Cambridge University Press.
Frith, S. (1988) 'Why do Songs have Words?', in *Music for Pleasure*, Polity.
Finnegan, R. (1988). *Literacy and Orality: Studies in the Technology of Communication*. Blackwell.
Goody, J. (2000) *The Power of the Written Tradition*, Smithsonian Institution Press.
Goody, J. (1972) *The Myth of the Bagre*, Clarendon Press.
Wagner, D. A. (ed) (1991) *Literacy. An International Handbook*, Westview.
[It is also worth revisiting the further reading for Chapter 2]

Chapter 6 Song. What comes first: words, music, or performance?

Berger, H. M. (1999) *Metal, Rock, and Jazz. Perception and the Phenomenology of Musical Experience*, Wesleyan University Press.
Feld, S. (1995) 'Wept thoughts: The Voicing of Kaluli Memories', in R. Finnegan and M. Orbell (eds) (1995) *South Pacific Oral Traditions*, Indiana University Press.
Feld, S. and Fox, A. A. (1994) 'Music and language', *Annual Review of Anthropology* 23: 25–53.
List, G. (1963) 'The boundaries of speech and song', *Ethnomusicology* 7, 1: 1–16.
Treitler, L. (2003) *With Voice and Pen. Coming to Know Medieval Song and How it was Made*, Oxford University Press.

Chapter 7 Competence and performance: Was Chomsky right after all?

Chomsky, N. (2008) *The Essential Chomsky*, Bodley Head.
Kendon, A. (2004) *Gesture: Visible Action as Utterance*, Cambridge University Press.
Verschueren, J. (2009) 'Introduction: The Pragmatic Perspective', in J. Verschueren and J.-O. Östman (eds) (2009) *Key Notions for Pragmatics*, John Benjamins.

Chapter 8 Poem and story: The arts of dreaming and waking to sweet words

Burke, P. (1997) 'The cultural history of dreams', in P. Burke, *Varieties of Cultural History*, Cornell University Press.

Edgar, I. (1999) 'Dream fact and real fiction: The realisation of the imagined self', *Anthropology of Consciousness* 10 (1): 28–42.

Farrar, C. (2012) *Li'l Ole Lil the Heavenly Rocker Makes Merry Heaven and Hell*, The Callender Press.

Pope, R. (2005) *Creativity: Theory, History, Practice*, Routledge.

Tedlock, B. (ed.) (1987) *Dreaming: Anthropological and Psychological Interpretations*, School of American Research Press.

Chapter 9 Where is literature?

Gerstle, A., Jones, S. and Thomas, R. (eds) (2005) 'Performance literature', special issue, *Oral Tradition* 20, 1–2.

Widdowson, P. (1999) *Literature*, Routledge.

BIBLIOGRAPHY

Abraham, K. (1979), 'Dreams and Myths: A Study in Folk Psychology', in *Clinical Papers and Essays on Psychoanalysis*, London: Hogarth Press.

Adorno, T. (1976) *Introduction to the Sociology of Music,* Eng. trans, New York: Seabury Press.

—(1991) *The Culture Industry*, J. Bernstein (ed.), London: Routledge.

Adorno, T. and Horkheimer, M. (1979) *The Dialectic of the Enlightenment*, London: Verso.

Allen, L. (1993) *Women Do This Every Day: Selected Poems of Lillian Allen*, Toronto: Women's Press.

Andrzejewski, B. W. (1985) 'Oral Literature', in B. W. Andrzejewski, S. Pilaszewicz and W. Tyloch (eds*) Literatures in African Languages*, Cambridge and Warsaw: Cambridge University Press and Wiedza Powszechna.

Asher, R. E. and Simpson J. M. Y. (eds) (1994) *The Encyclopedia of Language and Linguistics*, Oxford: Pergamon.

Askew, K. M., 2002, *Performing the Nation: Swahili Music and* Cultural Politics in Tanzania, Chicago: University of Chicago Press.

Astle, T. (1784) *The Origin and Progress of Writing*, London: The Author.

Austin, J. L. (1962) *How to Do Things with Words*, Oxford: Clarendon Press.

Bakhtin, M. M. (1973) *Problems of Dostoevsky's Poetics*, Ann Arbor: Ardis.

—(1981) *The Dialogic Imagination*, Eng. trans., Austin: University of Texas Press.

—(1986) *Speech Genres and Other Late Essays,* Eng. trans., C. Emerson and M. Holquist (eds), Austin: University of Texas Press.

Banti, G. and Giannatasio, F. (2004) 'Poetry', in A. Duranti (ed.), *A Companion to Linguistic Anthropology*, Oxford: Blackwell.

Barber, K. (1999) 'Quotation in the constitution of Yorùbá oral texts', *Research in African Literatures* 30.3: 17–41.

—(2003) 'Text and performance in Africa', *Bulletin of the School of Oriental and African Studies* 66: 324–33.

—(2007) *Texts, Persons and Publics in Africa and Beyond*, Cambridge: Cambridge University Press.

Barber, K. and Farias P. F. de M. (eds) (1989) *Discourse and its Disguises. The Interpretation of African Oral Texts* (Birmingham University African Studies Series 1), Birmingham: Centre of West African Studies.

Basso, E., Ellen B. and Brown, Michael F. (1992) *Dreaming: Anthropological and Psychological Interpretations*, School of American Research Press.

Bauman, R. (1977) *Verbal Art as Performance*, Rowley, Mass: Newbury House.

—(1986) *Story, Performance, and Event*, Cambridge: Cambridge University Press.

—(1989) 'American folklore studies and social transformation: A performance-centered perspective', *Text and Performance Quarterly* 9.3: 175–84.

—(1992) 'Performance', in R. Bauman (ed.) (1992) *Folklore, Cultural Performances, and Popular Entertainment*, New York: Oxford University Press.

—(2001) 'Mediational performance, traditionalization, and the authorization of discourse', in H. Knoblauch and H. Kotthoff (eds) *Verbal Art across Cultures. The Aesthetics and Proto-Aesthetics of Communication*, Tübingen: Narr.

—(2004) *A World of Others' Words. Cross-Cultural Perspectives on Intertextuality*, Oxford: Blackwell.

Bauman, R. and Briggs, C. L. (1990) 'Poetics and performance as critical perspectives on language and social life', *Annual Review of Anthropology* 19: 59–88.

—(2000) 'Language philosophy as language ideology: John Locke and Johann Gottfried Herder', in P. V. Kroskrity (ed.) *Regimes of Language. Ideologies, Polities, Identities*, Oxford: James Currey.

—(2003) *Voices of Modernity. Language Ideologies and the Politics of Inequality*, Cambridge: Cambridge University Press.

Bauman, R. and Sherzer, J. (eds) (1989) *Explorations in the Ethnography of Speaking*, 2nd edn, London: Cambridge University Press.

Bayly, A. (1789) *The Alliance of Musick, Poetry and Oratory*, London: John Stockdale.

Becker, H. S. (1982) *Art Worlds*, Berkeley, Los Angeles and London: University of California Press.

Ben-Amos, D. and Goldstein, K. S. (eds) (1975) *Folklore: Performance and Communication*, Berlin: Mouton de Gruyter.

Berger, H. M. (1999) *Metal, Rock, and Jazz. Perception and the Phenomenology of Musical Experience*, Hanover: Wesleyan University Press.

Berliner, P. (1976) 'The poetic song texts accompanying the *mbira dzavadzimu*', *Ethnomusicology* 20, 3: 451–82.

Biddle, J. L. (2002) 'The Warlpiri alphabet and other colonial fantasies', *Visual Communication* 1: 267–91.

Bloch, M. (1989) 'Literacy and enlightenment', in K. Schousboe and M. T. Larsen (eds) *Literacy and Society*, Copenhagen: Akademisk Forlag.

Boone, E. H. and Mignolo, W. D. (eds) (1994) *Writing Without Words. Alternative Literacies in Mesoamerica and the Andes*, Durham: Duke University Press.

Bornat, J. (1989) 'Oral history as a social movement', *Oral History* 17: 11–32.

Bourdieu, P. (1984) *Distinction*, English trans., London: Routledge.

Boyarin, J. (ed.) (1993) *The Ethnography of Reading*, Berkeley: University of California Press.

Brathwaite, E. (1984) *History of the Voice*, London: New Beacon Books.

Brown, C. S. (1948) *Music and Literature. A Comparison of the Arts*, Athens, GA: University of Georgia Press.

Brown, D. (2003) '"Where shall I wonder under the thunder who's that black boys making that black noise step a little closer to the mike": Prophets of da City and Urban South African Identity', in J. Draper (ed.), *Oral Literacy and Colonialism in Southern Africa*, Pietermaritzburg: De Volkstem.

—(ed.) (1999) *Oral Literature and Performance in Southern Africa*, Oxford: James Currey.

Brown, M. (1998) *The British Library Guide to Writing and Scripts: History and Techniques*, London: British Library.

Brown, S. (1987) 'Dub poetry: Selling out', *Poetry Wales* 22: 51–4.

Bruner, J. (1987) 'Life as narrative', *Social Research* 51: 1–32.

—(2002) *Making Stories*, Cambridge MA: Harvard University Press.

Bulkeley, K., Adams, K. and Davis, P. M. (eds) *Dreaming in Christianity and Islam: Culture, Conflict, and Creativity*, New Brunswick, USA: Rutgers University Press.

Burke, K. (1941) 'Literature as equipment for living', in *The Philosophy of Literary Form: Studies in Symbolic Action*, Baton Rouge: Louisiana State University Press.

Burke, P. (1997) 'The cultural history of dreams', in P. Burke, *Varieties of Cultural History*, New York: Cornell University Press.

Burnett, J. (ed.) (1974) *Useful Toil. Autoboiographies of Working People from the 1820s to the 1920s*, London: Allen Lane.

—(1982) *Destiny Obscure*, London: Allen Lane.

Burrows, D. (1990) *Sound, Speech, and Music*, Amherst: University of Massachusetts Press.

Cancel, R. (2004) 'Oral performance dynamics', in P. M. Peek and K. Yankah (eds) *African Folklore. An Encyclopedia*, New York: Routledge.

Carrier, J. and Carrier, A. (1995) 'Every picture tells a story: Visual alternatives to oral tradition in Ponam society', in R. Finnegan and M. Orbell (eds) *South Pacific Oral Traditions*, Bloomington: Indiana University Press.

Carruthers, M. (1990) *The Book of Memory*. Cambridge: Cambridge University Press.

Casas, M. C. de la (1998) 'Orality and literacy in a postcolonial world', *Social Semiotics* 8: 5–24.

—(2002) 'Multimodality in the poetry of Lillian Allen and Dionne Brand: A social semiotic approach', doctoral thesis, Institute of Education, University of London.

Case, S.-E., Brett, P. and Foster, S. L. (eds) (1995) *Cruising the Performative: Interventions into the Representation of Ethnicity, Nationality, and Sexuality*, Bloomington: Indiana University Press.

Cavallo, G. and Chartier, R. (eds) (1999) *A History of Reading in the West*, Cambridge: Polity.

Cavicchi, D. (1998) *Tramps Like Us: Music and Meaning Among Springsteen Fans*, New York: Oxford University Press

Certeau, M. de (1984) *The Practice of Everyday Life*, Berkeley, Los Angeles and London: University of California Press.

Chimombo, S. (1988) *Malawian Oral Literature: The Aesthetics of Indigenous Arts*, Zomba and London: Centre for Social Research, University of Malawi.

Chomsky, N. (2008) *The Essential Chomsky*, London: Bodley Head.

—(2011), 'Language and other cognitive processes', www.youtube.com/watch?v=6i_W6Afed2k (accessed 7 November 2014).

Clark, H. H. (1992) *Arenas of Language Use*, Chicago: University of Chicago Press.

—(1996) *Using Language*, Cambridge: Cambridge University Press.

Classen, C. (1997) 'Foundations for an anthropology of the senses', *International Social Science Journal* 153: 401–12.

Clayton, M., Herbert, T. and Middleton, R. (eds) (2003) *The Cultural Study of Music: A Critical Introduction*, New York: Routledge.

Clegg, S. R. (1993) 'Narrative, power, and social theory', in P. K. Mumby (ed.) *Narrative and Social Control*, London: Sage.

Clifford, J. and Marcus, G. (1986) *Writing Culture: The Poetics and Politics of Ethnography*, Berkeley: University of California Press.

Coleman, J. (1996) *Public Reading and the Reading Public in Late Medieval England and France*, Cambridge: Cambridge University Press.

Cooper, C. (1995) *Noises in the Blood. Orality, Gender, and the 'Vulgar' Body of Jamaican Popular Culture*, Durham: Duke University Press.

Cooper, C. and Devonish, H. (1995) 'A Tale of Two States: Language, Lit/orature and the two Jamaicas', in S. Brown (ed.) *The Pressures of the Text: Orality, Texts and the Telling of Tales*, Birmingham: Birmingham University African Studies Series 4.

Cope, B. and Kalantzis, M. (2000) (eds) *Multiliteracies*, London: Routledge.

Coplan, D. B. (1994) *In the Time of Cannibals. The Word Music of South Africa's Basotho Migrants*, Chicago: University of Chicago Press.

Cronon, W. (1992) 'A place for stories', *Journal of American History* 78: 1347–75.

Cummings, L. (ed.) (2010) *The Routledge Pragmatics Encyclopedia*, London: Routledge.

DeMaria, R. and Kitzinger, R. (eds) (1989) 'Transformations of the word', special issue, *Language and Communication* 9, 2/3.

Deal, T. E. and Kennedy, A. A. (1989) *Corporate Cultures*, Harmondsworth: Penguin.

Devereux, G. (1969) *Reality and Dream. Psychotherapy of a Plains Indian*, New York, International Universities Press.

Diamond, E. (ed.) (1996) *Performance and Cultural Politics*, London: Routledge.

Diringer, D. (1968) *The Alphabet. A Key to the History of Mankind*, 2 vols, 3rd edn, London: Hutchinson.

dos Santos, I. M. (2004) 'Literatura de cordel: Literature for Market and Voice', in M. J. Valdés and D. Kadir (eds) *Literary Cultures of Latin America. A Comparative History*, vol. 1, Oxford: Oxford University Press.

Draper, J. A. (ed.), *Orality, Literacy, and Colonialism in Antiquity*, Atlanta: Society of Biblical Literature.

Duranti, A. (1997) *Linguistic Anthropology*, Cambridge: Cambridge University Press.

—(ed.) (2001) *Key Terms in Language and Culture*, Oxford: Blackwell.

—(ed.) (2004) *A Companion to Linguistic Anthropology*. Oxford: Blackwell.

Duranti, A. and Goodwin, C. (eds) (1992) *Rethinking Context. Language as an Interactive Phenomenon*, Cambridge: Cambridge University Press.

Edgar, I. (1995) *Dreamwork, Anthropology and the Caring Professions: A Cultural Approach to Dreamwork*. Aldershot: Avebury.

—(1999) 'Dream fact and real fiction: The realisation of the imagined self', *Anthropology of Consciousness* 10 (1): 28–42.

—(2000) 'Cultural dreaming or dreaming cultures? The anthropologist and the dream', *KEA: Zeitschrift fur Kulturwissenschaften* 13: 1–20.

—(2003) 'Encountering the dream: Intersecting anthropological and psychoanalytical approaches', *Counselling and Psychotherapy Research* 3 (2): 95–101.

—(2008) 'The inspirational night dream in the motivation and justification of jihad', *Left Curve* 32: 27–34.

—(2009) 'A comparison of Islamic and Western psychological dream theories', in Bulkeley, K. *et al.* (eds) *Dreaming in Christianity and Islam: Culture, Conflict, and Creativity*, New Brunswick, USA: Rutgers University Press.

—(2011) *The Dream in Islam: From Qur'anic Tradition to Jihadist Inspiration*. Oxford: Berghahn Papers.

Entwistle, J. (2000) *The Fashioned Body*, Cambridge: Polity.

Farrar, C. (2012a) *The Little Angel and Three Wisdoms*, Houston: SBPRA.

—(2012b) *Three Ways of Loving*, Milton Keynes: The Callender Press.

—(2012c) *Li'l Old Lil the Heavenly Rocker Makes Merry Heaven and Hell*, Milton Keynes: The Callender Press.

—(2012d) *The Dragon's Tale*, Milton Keynes: The Callender Press.

—(2012e) *The Wild Thorn Rose*, Milton Keynes: The Callender Press.

Featherstone, M. (ed.) (2000) *Body Modification*, London: Sage.

Feld, S. (1995) 'Wept thoughts: The voicing of Kaluli memories', in R. Finnegan and M. Orbell (eds) *South Pacific Oral Traditions*, Bloomington: Indiana University Press.

Feld, S. and Fox, A. A. (1994) 'Music and language', *Annual Review of Anthropology* 23: 25–53.

Feld, S., Fox, A. A., Porcello, T. and Samuels, D. (2004) 'Vocal Anthropology: From the Music of Language to the Language of Song', in A. Duranti (ed.) *A Companion to Linguistic Anthropology*. Oxford: Blackwell.

Fine, E. (1984) *The Folklore Text: From Performance to Print*, Bloomington: Indiana University Press.

Finnegan, R. (1967) *Limba Stories and Story-Telling*, Oxford: Clarendon Press.

—(1977) *Oral Poetry: Its Nature, Significance and Social Context*, Cambridge: Cambridge University Press; (1992) Bloomington: Indiana University Press, 2nd edn.

—(1988) *Literacy and Orality: Studies in the Technology of Communication*, Oxford: Blackwell.

—(1989) *The Hidden Musicians: Music-Making in an English Town*. Cambridge: Cambridge University Press; (2007) Middletown: Wesleyan University Press, 2nd edn.

—(1990) 'Tradition – but what tradition and tradition for whom?', *Oral Tradition 6*.

—(1992) *Oral Traditions and the Verbal Arts: A Guide to Research Practices*, London: Routledge.

—(1996) 'Personal narrative and urban theory in Milton Keynes', *Auto/Biography* 4: 13–23.

—(1998) *Tales of the City*, Cambridge: Cambridge University Press.

—(2002) *Communicating. The Multiple Modes of Human Interconnection*, London: Routledge; (2014) 2nd (expanded) edn.

—(2006) 'Which comes first: the words, the music or the performance? Conference paper Rio de Janeiro, May 2006 [in Portuguese translation] in C. N. de Matos, E. Travossos and F. T. de Medeiros. (eds) *Palavra Cantada: Ensaios sobre Poesia, Musica e Voz*, Rio de Janeiro: 7Letras.

—(2007) *The 'Oral' and Beyond. Doing Things with Words in Africa*. Oxford: James Currey; Chicago: Chicago University Press; Scottsville: University of KwaZulu-Natal Press.

—(2012) *Oral Literature in Africa*, 2nd (illustrated and expanded) edn, Cambridge: Open Book.

—(ed.) (forthcoming a) *Entrancement: Dreams, Telepathy and Imagination*, Cardiff: University of Wales Press.

—(forthcoming b) *Shared Minds: True Tales of Earth, Heaven and Human Consciousness*.

Finnegan, R. and Orbell, M. (eds) (1995) *South Pacific Oral Traditions*, Bloomington and Indianapolis: Indiana University Press.

Foley, J. M. (1995) *The Singer of Tales in Performance*, Bloomington: Indiana University Press.

—(2002) *How to Read an Oral Poem*, Urbana: University of Illinois Press.

—(ed.) (2003) 'Oral tradition: State of the art', special issue, *Oral Tradition* 18: 1–2.

Foley, W. (2003) 'Genre, register and language documentation in literate and preliterate communities', *Language Documentation and Description* 1: 85–98.

Franchetto, B. (2006) 'Ethnography in Language Documentation', in J. Gippert, N. Himmelmann and U. Mosel (eds) *Essentials of Language Documentation*, Berlin: Mouton de Gruyter.

Frith, S. (1988) 'Why do Songs have Words?', in *Music for Pleasure*, Cambridge: Polity.

—(1996/1998) *Performing Rites: Evaluating Popular Music*, Oxford: Oxford University Press.

—(ed.) (2004) *Popular Music. Critical Concepts in Media and Cultural Studies*, 4 vols, London: Routledge.

Furniss, G. (2004) *Orality. The Power of the Spoken Word*, Basingstoke: Palgrave Macmillan.

Gans, E. (1999) 'The little bang: The early origin of language', *Anthropoetics* 5, 1.

Gentili, B. and Paioni, G. (eds) *Oralitá: Cultura, Letteratura, Discorso*, Roma: Ateneo.

Gerstle, A. (2000) 'Performance literature: the traditional Japanese theatre as model', *Comparative Criticism* 22: 39–62.

Gerstle, A., Jones, S. and Thomas, R. (eds) (2005) 'Performance literature', special issue, *Oral Tradition* 20, 1–2.

Gippert, J., Himmelmann, N. and Mosel, U. (eds) (2006) *Essentials of Language Documentation*, Berlin: Mouton de Gruyter.

Glaser, M. and Pausch, M. (eds) (1994) *Caribbean Writers: Between Orality and Writing*, Amsterdam–Atlanta GA: Rodopi.

Goffman, E. (1981) *Forms of Talk*, Philadelphia: University of Pennsylvania Press.

Goody, J. (1972) *The Myth of the Bagre*, Oxford: Clarendon Press.

—(1977) *The Domestication of the Savage Mind*, Cambridge: Cambridge University Press.

—(1982) *Cooking, Cuisine and Culture*, Cambridge: Cambridge University Press.

—(1985) 'Oral Composition and Oral Transmission: The Case of the Vedas', in B. Gentili and G. Paioni (eds) *Oralitá: Cultura, Letteratura, Discorso*, Roma: Ateneo.

—(1986) *The Logic of Writing and the Organization of Society*, Cambridge: Cambridge University Press.

—(1987) *The Interface Between the Written and the Oral*, Cambridge: Cambridge University Press.

—(1993) *The Culture of Flowers*, Cambridge: Cambridge University Press.

—(1995) *The Expansive Moment. The Rise of Social Anthropology in Britain and Africa 1918-1970*, Cambridge: Cambridge University Press.

—(1996) *The East in the West*, Cambridge: Cambridge University Press.

—(1997) *Representations and Contradictions: Ambivalence Towards Images, Theatre, Fiction, Relics and Sexuality*, Oxford: Blackwell.

—(1998) *Food and Love. A Cultural History of East and West*, New York: Verso.

—(1999) 'The Implications of Literacy', in D. A. Wagner, R. L. Venezky and B. V. Street (eds) *Literacy. An International Handbook*, Boulder, CO: Westview.

—(2000) *The Power of the Written Tradition*, Washington: Smithsonian Institution Press.

—(2012) *Metals, Culture and Capitalism, An Essay on the Origins of the Modern World*, Cambridge: Cambridge University Press.

—(ed.) (1968) *Literacy in Traditional Societies*, London: Cambridge University Press.

Goody, J. and Gandah, S. W. D. K. (1980) *Une récitation du Bagré*, Paris: Armand Colin.

Goody, J. and Watts, I. (1963) 'The consequences of literacy', *Comparative Studies in Society and History* 5: 304–45.

Gorz, A. (1982) *Farewell to the Working Class*, English trans., London: Pluto.

Graff, H. J. (1982) 'The legacies of literacy', *Journal of Communication* 32: 12–26.

—(ed.) (1981) *Literacy and Social Development in the West*, Cambridge: Cambridge University Press.

Graves-Brown, M. (ed.) (2000*) Matter, Materiality and Modern Culture*, London: Routledge.

Gunner, L. (ed.) (1994) *Politics and Performance: Theatre, Poetry and Song in Southern Africa*, Johannesburg: Witwatersrand University Press.

Habekost, C. (1993) *Verbal Riddim. The Politics and Aesthetics of African-Caribbean Dub Poetry*, Amsterdam and Atlanta, GA: Rodopi.

Hanks, W. F. (1996) *Language and Communicative Practices,* Boulder, co: Westview Press.

—(1989) 'Text and textuality', *Annual Review of Anthropology* 18: 95–127.

Hardy, B. (1968) *Tellers and Listeners: Narrative Imagination,* London: Continuum.

Harrán, D. (1986) *Word-Tone Relations in Musical Though from Antiquity to the Seventeenth Century*, Neuheusen–Stuttgart: Hänssler-Verlag.

Harris, R. (1986) *The Origin of Writing*, London: Duckworth.

—(1987). *The Language Machine*, London: Duckworth.

—(1998*) Introduction to Integrational Linguistics*, Oxford: Pergamon.

—(2000) *Rethinking Writing*, London: Athlone Press.

Harris, R. and Wolf, G. (1998) *Integrational Linguistics. A First Reader.* Oxford: Pergamon.

Harris, W. (2009) *Dreaming and Experience in Classical Antiquity*, Harvard: Harvard University Press.

Haviland, J. B. (2001) 'Gesture', in A. Duranti (ed.) *Key Terms in Language and Culture*, Oxford: Blackwell.

Herndon, M. (1989) 'Song', in E. Barnouw et al. (eds) *International Encyclopedia of Communications,* vol. 4, New York: Oxford University Press.

Hesmondhalgh, D. and Negus, K. (eds) (2002) *Popular Music Studies,* London: Arnold.

Hill, J. and Irvine, J. (eds) (1993) *Responsibility and Evidence in Oral Discourse*, Cambridge: Cambridge University Press.

Himmelmann, N. (2006) 'Prosody in language documentation', in J. Gippert, N. Himmelmann and U. Mosel (eds) *Essentials of Language Documentation,* Berlin: Mouton de Gruyter.

Hobsbawm, E. and Ranger, T. (eds) (1983) *The Invention of Tradition*, Cambridge: Cambridge University Press.

Hodge, R. and Kress, G. (1993) *Language as Ideology*, 2nd edn, London: Routledge.

Hoggett, P. and Bishop, J. (1986) *Organizing Around Enthusiasms: Patterns of Mutual Aid in Leisure*, London: Comedia.

Honko, L. (ed.) (2000) *Textualization of Oral Epics*, Berlin and New York: Mouton de Gruyter.

Howes, D. (ed.) (1991) *The Varieties of Sensory Experience. A Sourcebook in the Anthropology of the Senses*, Toronto: University of Toronto Press.

Hunter, L. and Oumarou, C. E. (1998) 'Towards a Hausa verbal aesthetic: Aspects of language about using language', *Journal of African Cultural Studies* 11, 2: 157–70.

Hutchinson, R. and Feist, A. (1991) *Amateur Arts in the U.K.*, London: Policy Studies Institute.

Hymes, D. H. (1975) 'Breakthrough into Performance', in D. Ben-Amos and K. S. Goldstein (eds) *Folklore: Performance and Communication*, Berlin: Mouton de Gruyter.

—(1977) *Foundations in Sociolinguistics: An Ethnographic Approach*, London: Tavistock.

—(1996) *Ethnography, Linguistics, Narrative Inequality*, London: Taylor and Francis.

Inglis, F. (1993) *Cultural Studies*, Oxford and Cambridge: Blackwell.

Irvine, J. (1996) '"Shadow Conversations": The Indeterminacy of Participant Roles', in M. Silverstein and G. Urban (eds) (1996) *Natural Histories of Discourse*, Chicago: University of Chicago Press.

Ivey, D. (1970) *Song. Anatomy, Imagery, and Style*, New York: Free Press.

Jannidis, F. et al. (eds) (2003) *Regeln der Bedeutung. Zur Theorie der Bedeutung literarischer Texte*, Berlin: Mouton de Gruyter.

Jedrej, M. and Shaw, R. (eds) (1992), *Dreaming, Religion and Society in Africa*, Leiden: Brill.

Johnson, B. (2000) *The Inaudible Music. Jazz, Gender and Australian Modernity*, Sydney: Currency Press.

Kaschula, R. H. (2003) 'Imbongi to slam: The emergence of a technologised auriture', *Southern African Journal for Folklore Studies* 14 (2): 46–58.

Keil, C. and Feld, S. (1994) *Music Grooves*, Chicago and London: University of Chicago Press.

Kendon, A. (2004) *Gesture: Visible Action as Utterance*, Cambridge: Cambridge University Press.

—(ed.) (1990) 'Conducting Interaction. Patterns of Behavior' in *Focused Encounters*, Cambridge: Cambridge University Press.

King, J. (2001) 'Text Setting', in S. Sadie (ed.) *The New Grove Dictionary of Music and Musicians*, 2nd edn, vol. 23, pp. 319–20.

Kittay, J. and Godzich, W. (1987) *The Emergence of Prose. An Essay in Prosaics*, Minneapolis: University of Minnesota Press.

Klassen, D. H. (2004) 'Gestures in African Oral Narrative', in P. M. Peek and K. Yankah (eds) *African Folklore. An Encyclopedia*, New York: Routledge.

Kotthoff, H. (2001) 'Aesthetic Dimensions of Georgian Grief Rituals: On the Artful Display of Emotions in Lamentation', in H. Knoblauch and H. Kotthoff (eds) *Verbal Art Across Cultures. The Aesthetics and Proto-Aesthetics of Communication*, Tübingen: Narr.

Kracke, W. (1987a), 'Myths in Dreams, Thought in Images: An Amazonian Contribution to the Psychanalytic Theory of Primary Process', in B. Tedlock (ed.)

Dreaming: Anthropological and Psychological Interpretations, Santa Fe: School of American Research Press.

—(1987b) 'Selfhood and Discourse in Sambia Dream Sharing', in B. Tedlock (ed.) *Dreaming: Anthropological and Psychological Interpretations*, Santa Fe: School of American Research Press.

Kramer, L. (1984) *Music and Poetry. The Nineteenth Century and After*, Berkeley: University of California Press.

Kress, G. (2002) *Literacy in the New Media Age*, London: Routledge.

Kwint, M., Breward, C. and Aynsely, J. (eds) (1999) *Material Memories. Design and Evocation*, Oxford: Berg.

Laing, D. (1990) 'Making Popular Music: The Consumer as Producer', in A. Tomlinson (ed.), *Consumption, Identity and Style: Marketing, Meanings and the Packaging of Pleasure*, London: Routledge.

Lash, S. and Friedman, J. (eds) (1992) *Modernity and Identity*, Oxford: Blackwell

Lefebvre, H. (1991) *Critique of Everyday Life*, London: Verso.

Linde, C. (1993) *Life Stories. The Creation of Coherence,* Oxford: Oxford University Press.

List, G. (1963) 'The boundaries of speech and song', *Ethnomusicology* 7, 1: 1–16.

Lohmann, R. I. (ed.) (2003) *Dream Travelers: Sleep Experiences and Culture in the Western Pacific*, New York: Palgrave Macmillan.

Lord, A. (1960) *The Singer of Tales*, Cambridge, MA: Harvard University Press.

Mannheim, B. and Tedlock, D. (eds) (1995) *The Dialogic* Emergence of Culture, Urbana: University of Illinois Press.

Matos, C. N. de (2004) 'Brazil's indigenous textualities', in M. J. Valdés and D. Kadir (eds) *Literary Cultures of Latin America. A Comparative History*, vol. 1, Oxford: Oxford University Press.

Matos, C. N. de, Travassos, E. and de Medeiros, F. T. (eds) (2008) *Palavra Cantada: Ensaios sobre Poesia, Musica e Voz*, Rio de Janeiro: 7 Letras.

McClellan, M. E. (1995) '"If we could Talk with the Animals": Elephants and Musical Performance during the French Revolution', in S.-E. Case, P. Brett and S. L. Foster (eds) *Cruising the Performative: Interventions into the Representation of Ethnicity, Nationality, and Sexuality*, Bloomington: Indiana University Press.

McLuhan, M. (1967) *Understanding Media, the Extensions of Man*, London: Sphere Books.

McNeill, D. (ed.) (2000) *Language and Gesture*, Cambridge: Cambridge University Press.

Menezes Bastos, R. J. de (1999) 'The "origin of samba" as the invention of Brazil (why do songs have music?)', *British Journal of Ethnomusicology* 8: 67–96.

Moraes, J. G. V. de (2008) 'Cantar e contar o coridiano; as Modhinas Paulistanas (anos 20/30)', in C. N. de Matos, E. Travassos and F. T. de Medeiros (eds) *Palavra Cantada: Ensaios sobre Poesia, Musica e Voz*, Rio de Janeiro: 7 Letras.

Morley, D. (1993) 'Active audience theory: Pendulums and pitfalls', *Journal of Communication* 43, 4: 13–19.

Morris, M. (1999) *'Is English We Speaking' and Other Essays*, Kingston: Randle.

Moyo, S. P. C. (1986) 'The Aesthetic Structure of Oral Poetry: The Media of a Complex Form', in S. P. C. Moyo et al. (eds) *Oral Traditions in Southern Africa*, vol. 4, Lusaka: Institute of African Studies, University of Zambia, pp. 482–515.

Moyo, S. P. C., Sumaili, T. W. C. and Moody, J. A. (eds) *Oral Traditions in Southern Africa*, vol. 4, Lusaka: Institute for African Studies, University of Zambia.

Mumby, P. K. (ed.) (1993) *Narrative and Social Control*, London: Sage.

Myerhoff, B. (ed.) (1980) *Number Our Days*, New York: Simon and Schuster.

Njogu, K. (1997) 'On the polyphonic nature of the Gicaandi genre', *African Languages and Cultures* 10: 47–62.

Nketia, J. H. K. (1996) 'National Development and the Performing Arts of Africa', in G. Altbach and S. M. Hassan (eds) *The Muse of Modernity. Essays on Culture as Development in Africa*, Trenton, NJ and Asmara Eritrea: Africa World Press.

O'Hanlon, M. (1983) 'Handsome is as handsome does: Display and betrayal in the Wahgi', *Oceania* 53: 317–33.

Okome, O. (1995) 'The character of popular indigenous cinema in Nigeria', *Ufahamu* 23, 2: 93–108.

Okpewho, I. (1979) *The Epic in Africa. Toward a Poetics of the Oral Performance*, New York: Columbia University Press.

—(1992) *African Oral Literature: Backgrounds, Character, and Continuity*, Bloomington: Indiana University Press.

—(2004) 'Oral Literary Research in Africa', in P. M. Peek and K. Yankah (eds) *African Folklore. An Encyclopedia*, New York: Routledge.

Olson, D. R. and Torrance, N. (eds) (2001) *The Making of Literate Societies*, Oxford: Blackwell.

Olson, D. R. and Kamawar, D. (2002) 'Writing as a Form of Quotation', in J. Brockmeier, M. Wang and D. R. Olson (eds) *Literacy, Narrative and Culture*, Richmond: Curzon.

Ong, W. (1944) 'Historical backgrounds of Elizabethan and Jacobean punctuation theory', *Publications of the Modern Language Association of America* 59: 349–60.

—(1982) *Orality and Literacy: The Technologizing of the Word*, London: Methuen.

Opland, J. (1998) *Xhosa Poets and Poetry*, Cape Town: David Philip.

Orwin, M. (2003) 'On the concept of "definitive text" in Somali poetry', *Bulletin of the School of Oriental and African Studies* 66, 3: 334–47.

Ottenberg, S. (1996) *Seeing with Music. The Lives of Three Blind African Musicians*, Seattle: University of Washington Press.

Pahl, K., Bullivant, D., Escott, H., Hodson, J., Hyatt, D., Hurcombe, M., Pool, S. and Steadman-Jones, R. (2013) *Language as Talisman*, AHRC Scoping study http://www.ahrc.ac.uk/Funding-Opportunities/Research-funding/Connected-Communities/Scoping-studies-and-reviews/Documents/Language%20as%20Talisman.pdf (accessed 1 July 2014)

Passerini, L. (1990) *Memory and Totalitarianism*, Oxford: Oxford University Press.

Peek, P. M. and Yankah, K. (eds) (2004) *African Folklore. An Encyclopedia*, New York: Routledge.

Penfield, J. (1983) *Communicating With Quotes: The Igbo Case*, London: Greenwood Press.

Perri, A. (2001) 'Writing', in A. Duranti (ed.) *Key Terms in Language and Culture*, Oxford: Blackwell.

Personal Narratives Group (1989) *Interpreting Women's Lives*, Bloomington: Indiana University Press.

Pfeiffer, K. L. (2002) *The Protoliterary. Steps Toward an Anthropology of Culture*, Stanford: Stanford University Press.

Phelan, P. (1993) *Unmarked. The Politics of Performance*, London: Routledge.

Plummer, K, (1983) *Personal Lives*, Bloomington: Indiana University Press.

—(1995) *Telling Sexual Stories:* Power, Change and Social Worlds, London: Routledge.

Pope, R. (2005) *Creativity: Theory, History, Practice,* London: Routledge.

Potter, J. (1998) *Vocal Authority. Singing Style and Ideology,* Cambridge: Cambridge University Press.

—(ed.) (2000) *The Cambridge Companion to Singing,* Cambridge: Cambridge University Press.

Prince, G. (1989) 'Narrative', in E. Barnouw et al. (eds) *International Encyclopedia of Communications,* New York: Oxford University Press.

Ricks, C. (2002) *Allusion to the Poets,* Oxford: Oxford University Press.

Riessman, C. K. (1993) *Narrative Analysis,* London: Sage.

Robinson, D. (2006) *Introducing Performative Pragmatics,* New York and London: Routledge.

Rosenwald, G. C. and Ochberg. R. L. (1992) *Storied Lives,* New Haven: Yale University Press.

Rubin, D. C. (1995) *Memory in Oral Traditions. The Cognitive Psychology of Epic, Ballads, and Counting-Out Rhymes,* Oxford: Oxford University Press.

Rumsey, A. (1990) 'Wording, meaning, and linguistic ideology', *American Anthropologist* 9: 346–61.

—(2001) 'Orality', in A. Duranti (ed.) *Key Terms in Language and Culture,* Oxford: Blackwell.

Saenger, P. (1997) *Space Between Words. The Origins of Silent Reading,* Stanford: Stanford University Press.

Sarbin, T. R. (1986) *Narrative Psychology,* New York: Praeger.

Schechner, R. (1988) *Performance Theory,* London and New York: Routledge.

Schechner, R. and Appel, W. (eds) (1990) *By Means of Performance,* Cambridge: Cambridge University Press.

Scheub, H. (1971) 'Translation of African oral-narrative performance to the written word', *Yearbook of Comparative and General Literature* 20, 28–36.

Schieffelin, E. L. (1998) 'Problematizing performance', in F. Hughes-Freeland (ed.) *Ritual, Performance, Media,* London: Routledge.

—(2003) 'Performance', in *Literature and Performance Email List,* discussion, 28 February 2003.

Schiffer, M. B. (1999) *The Material Life of Human Beings. Artifacts, Behavior, and Communication,* London: Routledge.

Schousboe, K. and Larsen, M. T. (eds) (1989) *Literacy and Society,* Copenhagen: Akademisk Forlag.

Scollon, R. (1999) 'Mediated Discourse and Social Interaction', in K. Tracey (ed.) 'Language and Social Interaction at the Century's Turn', special issue, *Research on Language and Social Interaction* 32, 1/2.

Seitel, P. (1980) *See So That We May See. Performances and Interpretations of Traditional Tales from Tanzania,* Bloomington: Indiana University Press.

Sell, K. (2005) *The Disciplines of Vocal Pedagogy: Towards A Holistic Approach,* Aldershot: Ashgate.

Sheldon, A. (1999) 'Approaching the future', in K. Tracey (ed.) 'Language and social interaction at the century's turn', special issue, *Research on Language and Social Interaction* 32, 1/2.

Sherzer, J. (1983) *Kuna Ways of Speaking. An Ethnographic Perspective,* Austin: University of Texas Press.

—(1990) *Verbal Art in San Blas. Kuna Culture Through its Discourse*, Cambridge: Cambridge University Press.

Shuman, A. (1986) *Storytelling Rights. The Uses of Oral and Written Texts by Urban Adolescents*. Cambridge: Cambridge University Press.

Silverstein, M. and Urban, G. (1996) *Natural Histories of Discourse*, Chicago: Chicago University Press.

Silverstone, R. (1994a) *Television and Everyday Life*, London and New York: Routledge.

—(1994b) 'The power of the ordinary: On cultural studies and the sociology of culture' [review essay], *Sociology* 28, 4, 991–1001.

—(1999) *Why Study the Media?* London: Sage.

Stanley, L. (1992) *The Auto-Biographical,* Manchester: Manchester University Press.

—(1993) 'On auto/biography in sociology', *Sociology*, 27, 1: 41–52.

Stevens, J. (1986) *Words and Music in the Middle Ages*, Cambridge: Cambridge University Press.

Stevenson, N. (1995) *Understanding Media Culture*, London, Sage.

Stone, R. M. (1998) 'Time in African Performance', in *The Garland Encyclopedia of World Music*, vol. 1, Africa, New York: Garland.

Storey, J. (ed.) (1996*) What is Cultural Studies?* London: Arnold.

Streeck, J. (1994) 'Gesture as communication II: The audience as co-author', in A. Kendon (ed.) (1994) 'Gesture and understanding in social interaction', special issue, *Research on Language and Social Interaction* 27, 3: 171–267.

Streeck, J. and Knapp, M. L. (1992) 'The Interaction of Visual and Verbal Features in Human Communication', in F. Poyatos (ed.) (1992) *Advances in Nonverbal Communication*, Amsterdam: Benjamins.

Street, B. (1984) *Literacy in Theory and Practice*, Cambridge: Cambridge University Press.

—(ed.) (1993) *Cross-Cultural Approaches to Literacy*, Cambridge: Cambridge University Press.

Swann, J., Pope, R. and Carter, R. (eds) (2011) *Creativity in Language and Literature: The State of the Art*, Basingstoke: Palgrave Macmillan.

Swift, G. (1983) *Waterland*, London: Heinemann.

Syed, M. (2011) *Bounce. The Myth of Talent and the Power of Practice*, London: Fourth Estate.

Tedlock, B. (ed.) (1987) *Dreaming: Anthropological and Psychological Interpretations*, Santa Fe: School of American Research Press.

Tedlock, D. (1972) *Finding the Center. Narrative Poetry of the Zuni Indians*, New York: Dial.

Thomas, R. (1989) *Oral Tradition and Written Record in Classical Athens*, Cambridge: Cambridge University Press.

Tonfoni, G. (1994) *Writing as a Visual Art*, Exeter: Intellect.

Tracey, K. (ed.) (1999) 'Language and social interaction at the century's turn', special issue, *Research on Language and Social Interaction* 32, 1/2.

Tran Quang Hai (2008) 'Acerca da noção de palavra falada e cantada no Vietnã', in C. N. de Matos, E. Travossos and F. T. de Medeiros (eds) *Palavra Cantada: Ensaios sobre Poesia, Musica e Voz*, Rio de Janeiro: 7 Letras.

Travassos, E. (2000) 'Ethics in the sung duels of North-Eastern Brazil: Collective memory and contemporary practice', *British Journal of Ethnomusicology* 9, 1: 61–94.

Treitler, L. (1984) 'Reading and singing: On the genesis of Occidental music-writing', *Early Music History* 4: 135–208.

—(2003) *With Voice and Pen. Coming to Know Medieval Song and How it was Made*, Oxford: Oxford University Press.

Turner, V. W. and Bruner, E. M. (eds) (1986) *The Anthropology of Experience*, Urbana and Chicago: University of Illinois Press.

Urban, G. (1984) 'Speech about speech in speech about action', *Journal of American Folklore* 97 (385): 310–28.

—(1988) 'Ritual wailing in Amerindian Brazil', *American Anthropologist* 90, 2: 385–400.

—(1991) *A Discourse-Centered Approach to Culture: Native South American Myths and Rituals*, Austin: University of Texas Press.

Valdés, M. J. and Kadir, D. (eds) (2004) *Literary Cultures of Latin America. A Comparative History*, 3 vols, Oxford: Oxford University Press.

Van Leeuwen, T. (1999) *Speech, Music, Sound*, Basingstoke: Macmillan.

Van Maanen, J. (1988) *Tales of the Field: On Writing Autobiography*, Chicago: University of Chicago Press.

Verschueren, J. (2009) 'Introduction: The Pragmatic Perspective', in J. Verschueren and J.-O. Östman (eds) *Key Notions for Pragmatics*, Amsterdam: John Benjamins.

Verschueren, J. and Östman, J.-O. (eds) (2009) *Key Notions for Pragmatics*, Amsterdam: John Benjamins.

Vincent, D. (1981) *Bread, Knowledge and Freedom: Study of Nineteenth-Century Autobiography*, London: Routledge.

Voloshinov, V. N. [?Bakhtin, M.] (1973/96) *Marxism and the Philosophy of Language*, English trans., Cambridge MA: Harvard University Press.

Wagner, D. A. (ed) (1991) *Literacy. An International Handbook*, Boulder: Westview.

Wallis, R. and Malm, K. (1984) *Big Sounds from Small Peoples. The Music Industry in Small Countries*, London: Constable.

Walser, R. (1993) *Running with the Devil. Power, Gender, and Madness in Heavy Metal Music*, Hanover: Wesleyan University Press.

Waterman, C. A. (1988) 'Asiko, sakara and palmwine: Popular music and social identity in inter-war Lagos', *Urban Anthropology* 17: 229–58.

Wells, H. G. (1946) *A Short History of the World*, Harmondsworth: Penguin.

White, H. (1973) *Metahistory*, Baltimore: Johns Hopkins Press.

Widdowson, P. (1999) *Literature*, London and New York: Routledge.

Winn, J. A. (1981) *Unsuspected Eloquence. A History of the Relations between Poetry and Music*, New Haven: Yale University Press.

Wolf, W. (1999) *The Musicalization of Fiction. A Study in the Theory and History of Intermediality*, Amsterdam: Rodopi.

Wolff, J. (1983) *Aesthetics and the Sociology of Art*, London: Allen and Unwin.

Wolfreys, J. (2001) *Introducing Literary Theories. A Guide and Glossary*, Edinburgh: Edinburgh University Press.

Wolfreys, J., Robbins, R. and Womack, K. (2002) *Key Concepts in Literary Theory*, Edinburgh: Edinburgh University Press.

Woodley, K. (2004) 'Let the data sing: Representing discourse in poetic form', *Oral History* 32, 1: 49–58.

Yankah, K. (1989) *The Proverb in the Context of Akan Rhetoric*, New York: Peter Lang.

—(1995) *Speaking for the Chief*, Bloomington: Indiana University Press.

INDEX